The architecture of
xrange

Inspired
by constraints

The architecture of
xrange

Inspired
by constraints

Foreword	Aric Chen
Introduction	Aaron Betsky
Interview	James Moore McCown
Afterword	Grace Cheung
Edited	Oscar Riera Ojeda

OSCAR RIERA OJEDA
PUBLISHERS

Contents

Foreword — Aric Chen
Vernaculars of Globalization

To consider the work of XRANGE in a Taiwanese, or even East Asian, context requires placing it within the milieu of the era of globalization from which it emerged. Indeed, the studio in many ways arose from the euphoria of ever-dissolving borders and increasingly frictionless movement—of people, ideas and resources—whose inevitability seemed a foregone conclusion beginning in the 1990s. But as those expectations now unravel and unwind, yielding to a condition that has yet to fully play out, the work of XRANGE and its cohorts is worth reexamining as part of a post-globalization phenomenon now unfolding in different ways.

From its beginnings, XRANGE embodied globalization in an almost literal sense. It was co-founded in 2003 by Grace Cheung, a Chinese Malaysian schooled in Canada and the United States. After completing her studies at Columbia University in New York, Cheung eventually found her way in 1995 to that most archetypal of global practices, Rem Koolhaas's Office for Metropolitan Architecture (OMA), first at its Hong Kong office and then in Rotterdam. One thinks of OMA at the time as being a singular architectural decoder of the global condition, its farflung projects drawing from Koolhaas's notions of "junkspace" and the generic to articulate a world of seemingly unfettered banality—of cookie-cutter highrises, shopping malls and airport duty free shops—through new typologies of space.

However, to the extent that every action prompts an opposite reaction, an entirely predictable consequence of globalization was a renewed emphasis on the local. Perhaps globalization could not be stopped, but its homogenizing effects could be negotiated by a reassertion of local identity and, in architecture, a retrained focus on the discipline's site and contextual specificities. In following, new design strategies began to emerge—a kind of situated globalism that sought to sort globalization's architectural language into localized dialects.

This was a widespread phenomenon, but it was perhaps most noticeable in post-colonial geographies and aspiring global centers—often the same places—as they funneled swirls of international capital into iconic buildings referencing desert roses or stands of bamboo in place-making bids to differentiate themselves, and compete, in a flattened world. In East Asia, as elsewhere, such efforts at "glocalization" often relied on cultural cliches. But they also created new filters for examining more stratigraphic notions of locality in ways that expanded definitions of the vernacular.

Cheung and XRANGE are among the generation of younger firms that have been especially active in the latter. Based in Taipei, Cheung has been a keen observer of "the strange ways," as she's put it, of her adopted city. For her, the Taiwanese capital is not a city of temples and nation-building monuments. Instead, it is a kind of self-generating agglomeration, or collage, of signage-plastered streets and buildings, architectural chimeras (say, a temple housing a betelnut vendor and barber shop) and other accretions of structures and building elements showing an improvisational flair. While Cheung no doubt benefits from her fresh perspective as a relative newcomer to Taiwan, in her observations she is not alone. One also thinks of the architect Hsieh Ying-Chun and his explorations of informal and unauthorized architecture, or the curator-writer Roan Ching-Yueh's investigations of Taiwan's ubiquitous 7-11 convenience stores as urban infrastructure.

Throughout East Asia, in fact, one sees a fascination with urban vernaculars: the once neon-splashed streets and tower-on-podium typologies of Hong Kong, for example, or the informal urban villages in Shenzhen, with their "handshake buildings" cramped so close together that residents of neighboring structures can clasp each other from across the gaps in-between. There are the signage bedecked façades of Seoul that have prompted new tropes on urban iconography, and the shophouses of Singapore, and much of Southeast Asia, whose spatial organizations have metamorphosized into countless contemporized iterations.

Sometimes these typologies are the product of regulation, but just as often, they result from a lack of regulation in earlier periods of hurried development. (It's perhaps no coincidence that similarities can be seen amongst the urban vernaculars of Taiwan, Hong Kong, South Korea and Singapore; once labelled the "Asian Tigers," all four underwent comparable trajectories of economic and urban growth as part of the global systems of the 1950s to the 1990s.)

Indeed, Cheung seems most intrigued by cities as metabolic organisms with self-evolving capacities—the source of an authentic identity, if you will, versus a constructed one. Her term for this is urbanmatic (from "urban automatic"), and it implies a process that works both outside of human agency and as an expression, as she has said, of "the collective desires of people," with architecture mediating between the two.

And so in XRANGE's work—which can so far be found exclusively in Taiwan—one sees the informal window boxes, laundry hanging rods and other unauthorized features that festoon many of the island's building's translated into the expanded aluminum-mesh screen that XRANGE applied onto a building renovation. The intention was not to conceal but to transform, through layering, the dilapidated old façade underneath. Elsewhere, the studio has incorporated traces of memory in the historical urban images that emerge from the screening elements of the CC Hong Memorial Hall, or in the paving patterns whose pixelated gradients approximate the architectural evolution of a site, now called The Railway Department Park, whose precise material history, dating from the Qing dynasty through Taiwan's Japanese colonial and Nationalist eras, has been lost.

On another former railway site, XRANGE translated the rooflines of Taipei into a telescoping urban stage set with pixelated pavement, while the bustling energy of the Ximenting district became an energy flow diagram expressed in a parametrically generated pattern of triangles on the façade of a new hostel. Indeed, while computational design does not figure strongly in its practice, the fact that XRANGE came of age during the rise of digitization is evident in its use of patterns, which rationalize the seemingly irrational "urbanmatic" landscape in a way that embraces the latter. What's more, there is the whiff of a self-generated architecture in even the studio's non-urban projects. Located in natural settings, XRANGE's Ant Farm House and Beetle House lend the impression of simple boxes morphing with ever greater complexity, their forms generated from, respectively, an existing structure and the natural landscape to create unexpected interstitial spaces.

Cheung has referred to architects as "front line workers" in tackling the "growing pains" of cities and conditions that are perpetually in flux. To be sure, her and XRANGE's work come at an inflection point, a period of global transition whose localized impacts and responses will continue to shape and produce new forms of architecture. After all, contemporaneity is a moving target, its contours inscribed not from scratch, but in layers and accretions that are subject to forces from both near and far. Put another way, newness eventually becomes a vernacular, and vernaculars never develop in isolation. XRANGE and others show us this. And so as the narrative of contemporary architecture in Taiwan, and elsewhere, continues to unfold, we may find that the vernacular has always been global and the global has always been a vernacular.

Aric Chen is General and Artistic Director of the Nieuwe Instituut, the Netherlands' national museum and institute for architecture, design and digital culture, in Rotterdam. American-born, Chen previously served as Professor and Founding Director of the Curatorial Lab at the College of Design & Innovation at Tongji University in Shanghai; Curatorial Director of the Design Miami fairs in Miami Beach and Basel; Creative Director of Beijing Design Week; and Lead Curator for Design and Architecture at M+, Hong Kong, where he oversaw the formation of that new museum's design and architecture collection and program.

Introduction — Aaron Betsky
Mass Curving Through Thin Air:
XRANGE Opens Up Taiwanese Architecture

Wander through Wandering Walls, a small boutique hotel at the very southern tip of Taiwan, and you will find yourself dancing with concrete. What you think of as a material whose weight mandates a solidity to the structures it forms here curves and contorts itself through the air as undulating walls that enclose one space, then continue through the air, shaping gardens or providing shade, before diving back into the structure. Providing shelter from the winds that blow with force on the exposed site, as well as from the sun and from other guests, the wandering walls are finally also a form of calligraphy that spell out the character of this particular and peculiar retreat.

The author of these gestures made concrete is the Taipei-based architect Grace Cheung, Principal and co-founder of the firm XRANGE. She calls her approach to architecture one of "story form." Cheung's architecture starts in all cases with a concept, which might be a response to the site, to the wishes, biases, and dreams of the client, or to a condition she finds in the brief with which she is faced. From that idea, which expresses itself in the names she gives her projects (not just Wandering Walls, which actually became the name of the hotel, but, for instance, "Music Box," "Ant Farm," "Urban Code," and, most enigmatically, "Stone Cloud") she develops a form, which for her means a shape or container, often with an element of expression that signals the underlying concept. With the idea now concrete (in many cases quite literally, as it is her preferred building material), Cheung then develops a structural system that births a spatial hierarchy or sequence of spaces within the building. Rather than thinking from either inside out, or from context and precedent in, Cheung distills what she interprets as the essence of the situation, develops that into a spatial sign, and then articulates those design decisions into habitable spaces.

That the result is usually architecture that is both pleasant to inhabit and detailed with great care is something Cheung attributes both to her background and to her discernment, trained by years of working for others and in her own firm: "I have an eye of how the idea can be made material, and how they can then turn into a form of inhabitable sculpture," she explains. The confidence that attitude betrays belies the relative newness of her firm, as well as her strong ambitions.

The background that brought this architect to that position is part of the reason for her sense of purpose. Born and raised as a child in Malaysia, she moved to Winnipeg during high school and then attended the University of Manitoba. A chance encounter with a book of black-and-white photographs of the

work of "modern masters" such as Le Corbusier and Ludwig Mies van der Rohe sent her on the path to architecture. After graduating from the University of Manitoba, she worked for John and Patricia Patkau, the Vancouver-based architects who have perfected architecture that draws on local materials, a strong attention to crafted details, and a highly developed sense of spatial sequence to create buildings with both strong imagery and beautifully developed spaces.

Cheung then moved to New York to obtain her graduate degree from Columbia University and worked for the School's Dean, Bernard Tschumi. There she picked up her focus on concept and the notion that architecture is a way of framing and articulating an event—a set of social relations made manifest—into buildings whose structure and form shape a dramatic sense of place. Finally, Cheung went to Rotterdam to work for the central wizardry school of high modernism, the Office for Metropolitan Architecture. While she was there, the firm obtained its first commission in Asia, a rest area and food market along one of Taiwan's main highways. Because she spoke Mandarin, the firm sent her to Taipei to work on the job. While in Taipei, she met her future husband, the graphic and industrial designer Royce Hong. Together, they started XRANGE after obtaining the commission to design the trophy for the award initiated by Sir Run Run Shaw's Foundation. Initially focused on smaller design artifacts and projects (in a range that the two founders designated as unknown, or "x"), it soon bifurcated into Royce's entrepreneurial designs for everything from camera stands to batteries, and the architecture office Grace helms.

XRANGE continues, however, to combine an interest in the designs of objects that fall into the realm of industrial design, including furniture, with a portfolio of buildings that ranges from interior renovations and temporary installations all the way to office buildings and hotels. So far, they are all located in Taiwan, and Cheung insists that the work comes out of a response to the geology, climate, and culture of this island. Coming there as a foreigner, she has a sense of distance from the indigenous traditions, the imposition of various styles by a century of Japanese occupation, and the development of a modernism, often with a combination of abstracted Chinese elements and rather monumental uses of concrete, steel, and glass.

What she concentrates on instead is a response to immediate context, and to the climate, pointing out that "the weather

here is unforgiving; because of the humidity and the salinity, you are limited in what materials you can use and how you develop spaces." In addition, she respects and uses as a starting point feng shui principles, but also such givens as the strongly developed ceramic tile industry, which makes it a natural material to use in cladding, as well as the use of reinforced concrete as the almost inevitable main construction method. Cheung's work is part of the internationalization of Taiwan's architecture, which has been achieved both through the work of notable local architects, but also through the importation of well-known designers (including OMA) to design anchor and icon buildings throughout the island. XRANGE's axis, in other words, runs not only between different scales and approaches, but along the "glocal" in which a vernacular that comes out of local conditions accepts and expresses itself through global modes of expression and functioning.

Most of Cheung's early commissions came, as she points out, from "friends and family": the renovations and additions to her own firm, offices for her husband's various start-ups, and the business in which the Hong family (Royce's grandfather founded what is now Panasonic Taiwan) have an interest. This allowed her to test out her ideas and to have the freedom to experiment with materials, structures, and form.

Her own house, which she calls Ant Farm, is a case in point. Cheung and Hong found an old stone house on a slope overlooking Taipei. It was small, but in a good location. Rather than tearing the existing structure down, they transformed what had been a tight configuration of spaces into something that is more like a loft shot through with intersecting volumes and planes. The outside is no longer the modest ramble of most of its neighbors, but a three-story object rising as black-colored enigma behind a parking garage block (Hong is a collector of classic cars). The main object is split into striations of glass and stucco that indicate the major living spaces, and a secondary form shaped to reveal the main staircase.

After you enter through a narrow slot next to the garage, the house opens up into an expansive, but vertically constrained slot providing views up and into the living areas. The spaces inside are tallest at the front of the house, where large windows open up to the views and the staircase becomes the link between that metropolitan scene and the world of the family. That space is defined as a living area taking up the whole main floor of the existing house. Bedrooms and bathrooms above and in the margins of these rooms turn inward to create the greatest degree of privacy.

What makes this layering of spaces dramatic is the manner in which Cheung has turned every volume she could into an object that stands on its own, often hovering just inches away from a nearby wall or ceiling, while deforming these pieces to adjust them to their functional and structural reality. The walls of the original house, revealed in their full thickness, as all windows and doors have been removed, are whitewashed, placing them in contrast to the smooth, white surfaces of the new additions. Wood details in the railings, doors, and sections of wall provide moments of sensuality in the otherwise abstract play of spaces and forms, while the black-painted steel columns and beams that make all this possible frame these compositions both visually and literally.

At an even smaller scale, Cheung designed a variety of different furniture pieces for the Ant House. These range from specifications of the "saddlebag" spaces (as the architect Charles Moore dubbed the small volumes that hang off the larger ones) that make use of the slots between old and new structures for little nooks and crannies outfitted with desks, shelves, and closets, to the massive conversation pit with its bullnosed profile that defines the living area. The architect learned from these constructions, and now delights in offering furniture for her commissions where she can, while considering ways to mass produce her designs.

That sense of architecture developing between the making of large, loft-like spaces framed by expressive structure and stairs treated as sculptural elements, and then proceeding into separate surface treatments and built-in furniture, has become a mainstay of Cheung's residential renovations, stores, and small offices. The two offices she has designed for her husband's start-up companies, Ipevo and Xing, are particularly inventive.

At the offices for Ipevo, her touch was light, but graphically vivid. Some walls are covered with drawable slate, so that messages to clients and the design and sales team can be scribbled on them. Even more dramatic are other wall and ceiling panels that are made of artificial grass woven into steel mesh. These elements, along with a few wood accents and graphics spelling out the company name, stand in contrast to an office space Cheung left largely as she found it, with white-painted walls and ceilings, a concrete floor, and simple metal fixtures. The space translates the scissoring arms and grips of the company's product (designed to facilitate hands-free video meetings with mobile devices) into a spatial aesthetic, adding a sense of lightness and whimsy through the woven planes and graphics.

At Xing, a maker of electric batteries whose integral cooling technology is its key innovation, the effects are more dramatic. When you enter, you are confronted by blue and white directional signs such as you might find on the highway, with the arrows all pointing in different directions. The colors are mirrored in curtains around break-out spaces made out of recycled Tyvek, while the traffic motif, which plays on the company's name, comes back in orange reflective disks mounted on a metal frame to provide more moveable office divisions.

Xing's most dramatic element is a staircase, or rather two parallel and identical stairs that run on either side of a structural wall. Its balustrade is made out of recycled compressed wood chips, while the stairs themselves, as well as the handrails, are made of plywood. A blue bollard, set into the balustrade, acts as an accent. The composition is simple, but highly refined in its play of different textures of wood elements. The whole design emphasizes rough, readymade surfaces and materials, brought together for the maximum graphic and sensory impact. It is an object lesson in both "less is more," and in the formally minimal, but witty and sensorily rich aesthetic developed by OMA, carried out in a manner that will allow Xing to grow or change in place.

An even more personal and minimal project, and one that sums up much of what Cheung does at a small scale with both simple and luxurious materials, is the pavilion she designed for the Hong family graveyard outside of Taipei. The site consists of a series of terraces, each reserved for a different generation. The current heirs to this rather illustrious family will occupy a lower level, which is necessarily mainly empty. Here Cheung placed a rectangular grid of black-painted steel elements at the end of the long axis. An off-center pair of benches provide a place to "visit with our ancestors," as Cheung puts it, and a glass roof hovers above the structure to shelter them from the rain when they do so.

What makes the pavilion extraordinary is the "stone cloud" that gives the project its name: slabs of veined blue and white marble, suspended below the roof and arranged in off-setting diagonal patterns. These serve to provide shade, but they are also abstractions of the traditional tombs on site, cut into pieces and colored to catch the sun, mirror the often blue-and-white sky, and cast a continually changing pattern of shadows. It is architecture taken apart into its simplest elements, which are then used in a fashion that reverses our expectation of their natural place in relation to gravity and light, and recomposed in a manner that evokes the past, but opens it up to new uses and interpretations. It was not until Cheung had completed the design, she says, that she found out that her husband's father has referred to the cultural endeavors he helped fund as a "stone cloud" that floated above the work of the everyday with beauty and contradictory weight.

Cheung's work tends to contain or focus on such gestures which, at their best, combine a sculptural sensibility—she cites the work of Tony Cragg and Richard Serra as influences—with a conceptual clarity. They often make their point by defying our expectation of what a material should be, whether it is (fake) grass suspended overhead, a stone cloud, or concrete slicing through the air. She then combines these pieces with spaces that are as simple and open as she can make them, framing and modulating these rooms with structure that she expresses as forthrightly as possible and, at times, uses as the sculpture in the room.

These techniques are most obviously at work in her installations and public space designs. The "Cloud," for instance was a 2008 temporary work for a design event that floated a "sack of synthetic fibers" of nine hundred square meters over a square, transforming the public space into a gathering area whose light and even parameters changed continually as the cloud responded to wind and light. She has proposed a more permanent version of this ephemeral object in Urban Scope, a pavilion that is one of the additions she is proposing as part of the redevelopment of a large public square. Its cloud-like form also mirrors and abstracts the skyscrapers around it, while being expandable to accommodate different uses.

More permanent are Cheung's installations for the former Taipei Railroad Station, now a railway museum. There she added curved walkways with barrel vaulted wood ceilings snaking between the site's various buildings, as well as perimeter fences made of concrete posts, tightly spaced and high enough to deter entrance, that are perforated with a computer pattern to allow for a sense of openness and rhythm. A

be obscured by adjacent development) with a curving glass façade. Recalling Ludwig Mies van der Rohe's Friedrichstrasse skyscraper project of 1921, the undulations dissolve the building's bulk, while also providing variety within the office floors inside. At the Winbond Building's base is a stand-alone auditorium, whose interior is formed by rows of wood trusses that intersect to evoke the Chinese character for rice, while weaving a nest of wood that turns the space into a large cocoon. The effect was originally meant to be even stronger because Cheung designed the structure to support an integrated roof, but regulations made her add an adjacent shell.

The building that most clearly combines the conceptual or contradictory treatment of weight, structure, and sign that mark Cheung's work is the private home she designed on the Penghu Peninsula for a bubble tea franchise magnate who is originally from the islands. The building presents itself as a wave rising up out of a mixed agricultural and residential neighborhood. That image certainly evokes the surrounding ocean, which the owners can see from their top-level bedroom, but also Penghu's vernacular of courtyard houses, with their coral stone walls and tile roofs that rise in undulating versions of the traditional Chinese curved gable. Clad in stone, the house appears massive on three sides, with only thin slots giving a sense of its character. It is on the side facing the dunes and distant sea that the house opens up with glass walls, which Cheung kept back from the shell to protect the occupants from the strong winds that buffet the site.

Inside, the house internalizes, abstracts, and redefines the courtyard type. Instead of there being an outdoor space (or series of them) surrounded by pavilions occupied by different generations or for different uses, most of the house consists of one giant living area. The roof presents itself on the inside here as a canopy of wood slots that rises from the glass wall facing the outside to a clerestory above a balcony. To call this space a living room would be an understatement. It serves as the gathering point for several generations of the owner's extended family. Rooms for his parents and an ancestor shrine are tucked into the sides, while the principal bedroom retreats slightly from the hubbub below on the top floor. The whole ground floor consists of over-scaled rooms outfitted with mats so that up to eight members of the clan can sleep in each space. This is not so much a house as it is a calligraphic icon of family gathering, made into a grand space enlivened by the sculpture of the roof, and held together by a stone-clad concrete structure.

The most expressive of Cheung's work to date—XRANGE has quite a few projects on the boards—remains the Wandering Walls hotel. The structure is essentially a machine for sheltering the eight hotel rooms and the public spaces that make up this isolated retreat from the fierce winds that come over the China Sea, creating moments of respite that are still filled with light and open to views. Cheung accomplished her basic

ground pattern traces the site of now removed railroad lines and points towards gathering spots in the public space.

A few of Cheung's larger commissions have also given her a chance to integrate such moments of conceptual clarity and visual or material contradiction into otherwise standard buildings. The most extreme of these projects was the Music House, a concrete shell stacking up four stories in a Taipei neighborhood. What appears to be a solid structure is shot through with windows of different sizes and configurations. While some are square or rectangular, others are L-shaped or make a cross in the façade. Because of their spacing, the Music House's structure seems carved out to the point of near collapse, although the corners, as in almost all Cheung's designs, guarantee solidity. The inside was meant to be the most extreme spatial and sculptural puzzle the architect designed, containing multiple levels opening up to each other and wood-enclosed practice rooms for the musician couple who were meant to occupy the structure. Sadly, the two divorced before completion and the house now stands as an expressive ruin.

The Winbond Company building in the suburb of Zhubei wears its expressive moment as a cloak. An otherwise standard block is clad on two sides (the other sides will eventually goal by making a curved building that arcs to the view, and then weaving concrete walls in and out of that shape. These wandering perimeters enclose rooms, but also apses where a single tree stands in light, protected from the elements, stairs that connect the three floors, and pools and hot tubs. They vary from level to level, so that they sometimes crisscross in midair, giving you a view of what you think of as a heavy material curving freely through space.

From the outside, Wandering Walls recalls the Neo-Brutalist structures of the 1960s, but also, perhaps unconsciously, the nearby military installations that dot the area. The image is one of solidity and safety, but also of a sensuality that in its curvatures evokes both the landscape elements and bay in front of the building and the body as it moves through these sinuous rooms. On the inside, the walls curve in to stage your entry into the spaces, while wood ceiling panels, doors, and bedframes invite the touch wherever your body might come into contact with the architecture.

Although Wandering Walls' idea is simple, the intricacy of the design creates a variety of different views, compositions, and experiences throughout what is a very small space. The sense you have of being continuously enclosed and embraced by what should be a harsh material contrasts with continual openings to the wide open spaces around the hotel. Everywhere you look, the architecture composes itself in a new manner, and everywhere your eye and your body are invited to go exploring.

In this project, Cheung has developed a way to build her "story form" into a strategy that produces both an immediate response to the human body and a concept that that is evident in the unity of the building. She does this through abstraction and contradiction, using the structure necessary to shape spaces to create effects that open up, reverse, and confound your understanding of where you are and what you are experiencing. The result is architecture of bravura and panache that is rooted in her adopted home, both in terms of its geology and climate, and in how her design responds to vernacular traditions, whether in architecture and beyond.

As XRANGE's portfolio continues to grow, and Cheung develops her architecture in conjunction with the art-oriented programs that she helps sponsor through her family's Hong Foundation, the opportunities to express and draw striking form in the air will no doubt continue to increase. Cheung's practice has already brought a sense of both sculpture and controlled whimsy, as well as a spatial complexity, to a Taiwanese architecture scene that had too little of these qualities. She has achieved this in a relatively short time (in architecture years), and has marked XRANGE as a practice worth watching, not just in Taiwan, but on the international scene.

Aaron Betsky

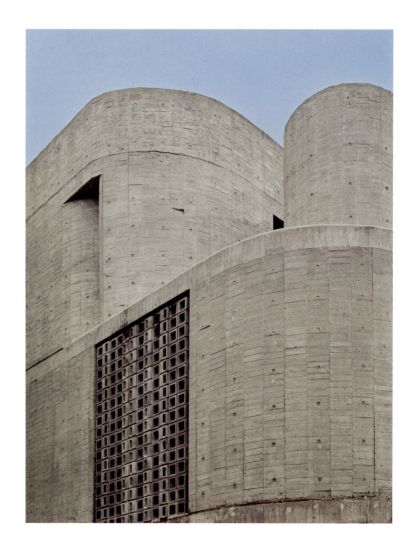

Aaron Betsky is Director of the School of Architecture and Design at Virginia Tech. Previously, he was President of the School of Architecture at Taliesin. A critic of art, architecture, and design, Mr. Betsky is the author of over twenty books on those subjects. He writes a twice-weekly blog for architect-magazine.com, Beyond Buildings. Trained as an architect and in the humanities at Yale University, Mr. Betsky has served as the Director of the Cincinnati Art Museum (2006-2014) and the Netherlands Architecture Institute (2001-2006), as well as Curator of Architecture and Design at the San Francisco Museum of Modern Art (1995-2001). In 2008, he also directed the 11th Venice International Biennale of Architecture. His latest books are *Fifty Lessons from Frank Lloyd Wright* (2021), *Making It Modern* (2019) and *Architecture Matters* (2019). His *Anarchitecture: The Monster Leviathan* will be published by The MIT Press in 2023.

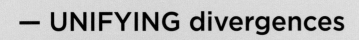
— **UNIFYING** divergences

Multiple constraints and disparate, complex requirements are solved by a simple, singular form strategy by these projects. **Wandering Walls** uses only walls that fold, curve and double back onto themselves, in response to the site's local construction culture, lack of budget or access and severe winds. **Urban Code Building** upends Taipei's building codes by maximizing design aspects previously unachievable, providing a large outdoor living space, north-south cross ventilation and natural light with a column-free interior. **Winbond Electronics Corporation** at once recalls Mies van der Rohe's seminal Friedrichstrasse tower from the 1920s, but with gentle curves derived from pockets of human-centric soft spaces, rejecting cold modernism to address the client's desire for workers' well being. Finally **The Cloud** is an unapologetic and delightful self-floating temporary canopy, the massive balloon space frame of 12 balloons reacts to the site's history, its intended transient use, ease of construction and climate responsiveness.

Wandering Walls
— A retreat where walls "wander"

On an ocean front mountain top between tall grasses and acacia forests, rugged curvaceous walls blur the boundaries between architecture and landscape to define public and private spaces of an 8 room retreat. The retreat, thus named Wandering Walls, is a building where the walls "wander" throughout like flowing ribbons.

The remote location is susceptible to gale-force winter winds, sea salt in the atmosphere, and had no access road prior to construction. Furthermore, the lack of skilled construction labor and the shoestring project budget drove the decision to use cast in place concrete early on at the concept phase for its climatic endurance, ease of transport and storage on site.

Inspired by the raw beauty of the natural surroundings, the design concept seeks to create a sense of quietude and permanence with a single architectural element and a minimal palette of materials; defining the entire architecture with just curves walls that are both structure and form, inside and outside, exterior and interior all at once.

The building hugs the edge of a native crop of acacia trees to gently curve out towards the ocean. In addition to providing essential wind shelter, the acacia forest becomes the entry experience. The building has no windows on the windward side, but opens up with floor to ceiling windows towards the expanse of hill top grasslands and spectacular sunsets over the ocean.

The flat slab and bearing wall structural system enables the concrete bearing walls to be misaligned vertically. The walls move in and out of the 3 floors independently, dictated by room layouts, views and the placements of wind barriers. At the stairs, curve walls hover over each other to reveal the horizon at the juncture of the sky, forest and ocean. The walls fly 4.5m off the

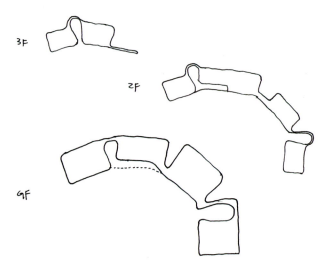

3F

2F

GF

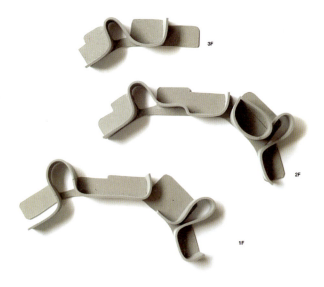

3F

2F

1F

SKETCHES

The architecture of **xrange**   Inspired by constraints

2F and 3F floor plates to form a vertical suspended enclosure, an echo chamber of sorts where the sound of acacia leaves rustling in the strong ocean winds is amplified. On the ground floor, the walls cantilever off the floor slab to form courtyards.

Local formwork made of recycled or rough low grade wood was used, 30cm wide panels for bigger curves, 20cm for tighter curves and 4cm batons for sharp curves. The highly tolerant formwork system allows for misalignments and mistakes made by the local workers, which created the signature "lo-res" curves throughout.

Along their entire lengths, the materiality of the curve walls transitions from rough concrete to wood, metal and tiles. Where the walls hover above ground to create courtyards, red earth stains become a part of the tactile landscape experience. On the windward side, the roughened cast textures of the walls has also gradually smoothed out due to their constant stripping by the seasonal winds.

On the roof is a 360 degree infinity pool with sweeping panoramic views of the ocean and the surrounding mountains. Supplied with fresh water filtered from an eco pond on the grounds without the use of chlorine and other harsh chemicals, birds can often be seen playing in the pool. The conservation of the acacia and surrounding grasslands is a primary aspect in the landscape design.

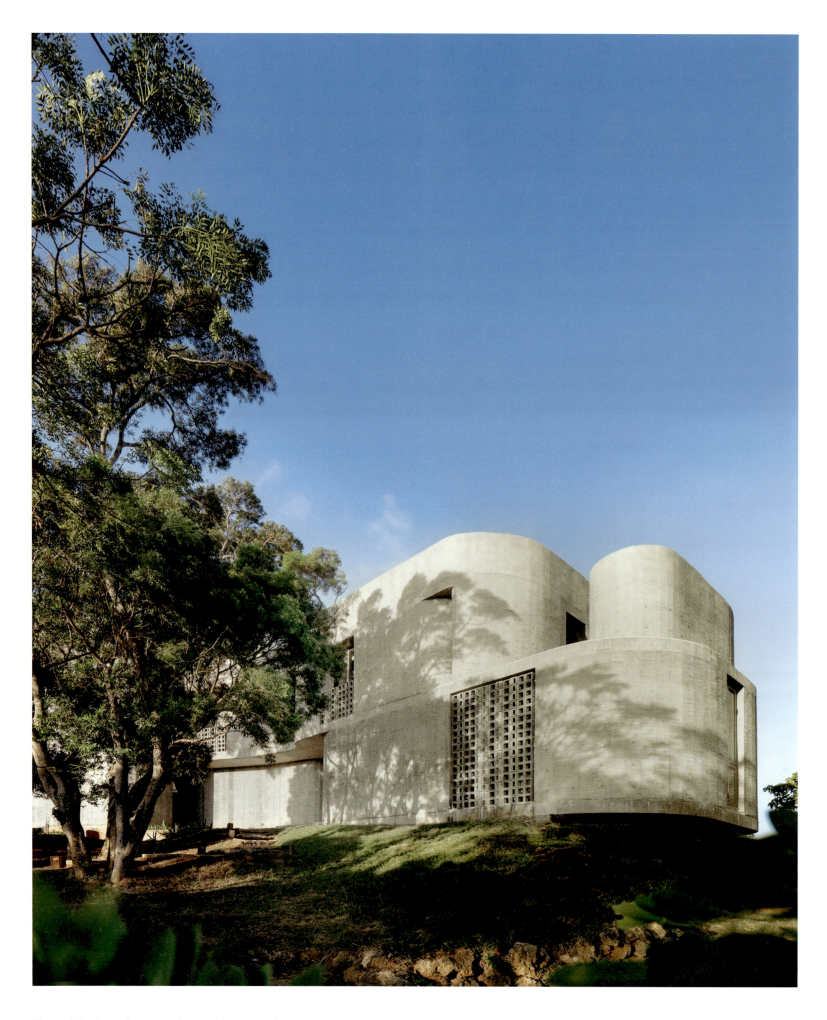

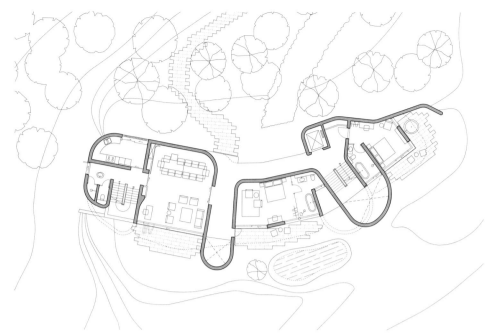

1F PLAN

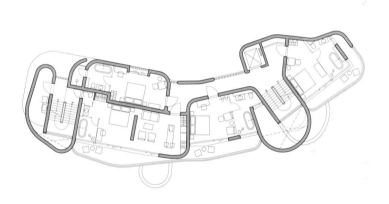

2F PLAN

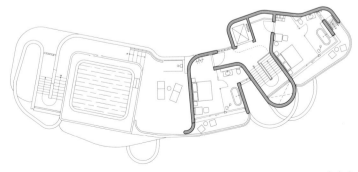

3F PLAN

0 1 2   5m   N

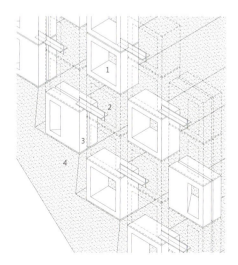

STAIR RAILING ASSEMBLY

1. 190x190x10mm concrete block
2. Cross shape stainless steel connector
3. Cement mortar
4. "Minshizi" washed pebble screed

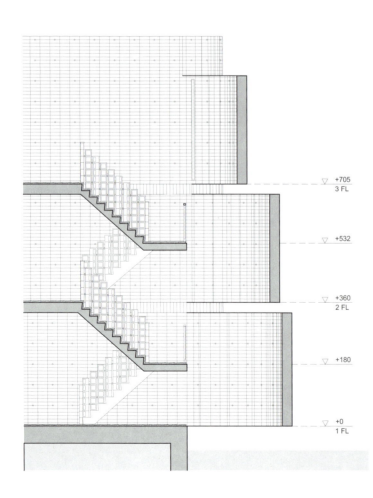

STAIR SECTION   0   0.5   1   2m

△ +705
3 FL

△ +532

△ +360
2 FL

△ +180

△ +0
1 FL

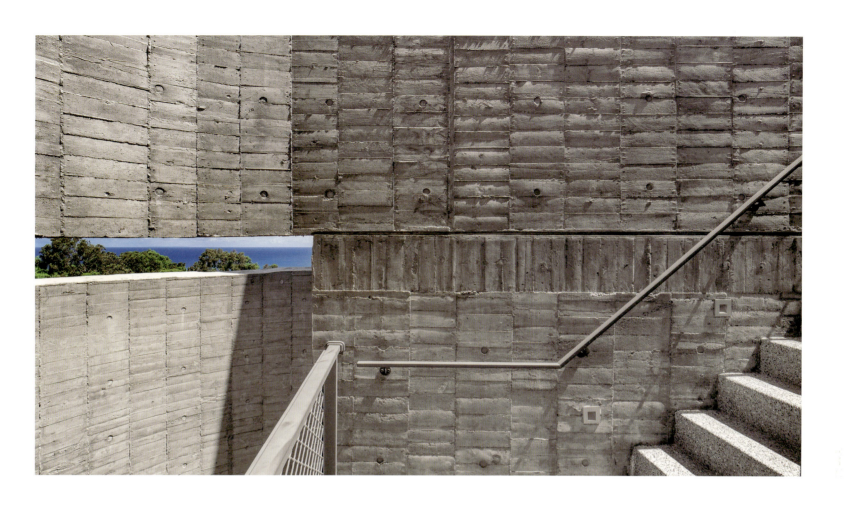

1F

1A   1C
1B

2F

2A   2D
2B   2C

3F

3C
3A   3B

FORMWORK SYSTEM

The architecture of **xrange**   Inspired by constraints

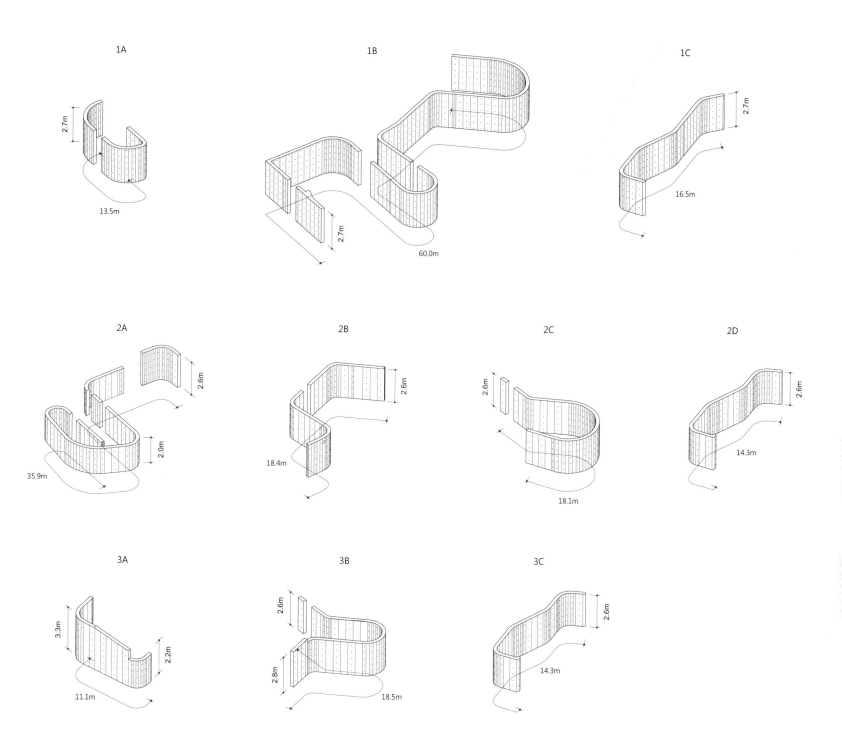

1A

2.7m

13.5m

1B

2.7m

60.0m

1C

2.7m

16.5m

2A

2.6m

2.0m

35.9m

2B

2.6m

18.4m

2C

2.6m

18.1m

2D

2.6m

14.3m

3A

3.3m

2.2m

11.1m

3B

2.6m

2.8m

18.5m

3C

2.6m

14.3m

Urban Code Building
— Urban housing typology rewired

On a dense urban site with meandering alleys, this 6 unit residential project turns 2 major tenets of local urban housing typology on its head.

Deeply influenced by the culture of feng shui, Taiwanese home owners are unequivocally biased towards rectilinear plan layouts without any columns protruding into the interior, or beams overhead of main spaces. With concrete framing system typically the construction of choice for small to mid size housing projects due to their lower costs, this has given rise to the prevalent practice of exposing the concrete structural frames on the outside envelopes of residential buildings, giving Taiwanese residential buildings their characteristic gridded frame exteriors. Furthermore, the building code allows a percentage area of canopies, balconies and planters to be exempted from the maximum gross floor area calculations, thereby making them freebie extra areas that developers can sell. As incentives of great benefits to developers, these free add-ons are essentially must-do for architects. As a result, gridded concrete frame exterior with various barnacle-like add-on articulations on the tower form become the de facto residential typology here.

First, to upend the above ubiquitous convention for housing, and to achieve a building envelope without any protruding concrete structural frames, a hybrid structural system is developed. Three 30cm thick load bearing walls, reinforced by cross walls at the elevator core, form the parti organization. Spanning 12m in between is a 30cm thick concrete floor slab, a portion of which is sunken and reinforced at the edges with edge beams and a single steel column. Constrained within a floor to floor height of 330cm, the hybrid structural system creates a large column free residential unit interior of 12m x 11m. The units' service areas are furthermore integrated into the core, giving the units a squarish column-free open plan and a north south transparency best for lighting and natural ventilation.

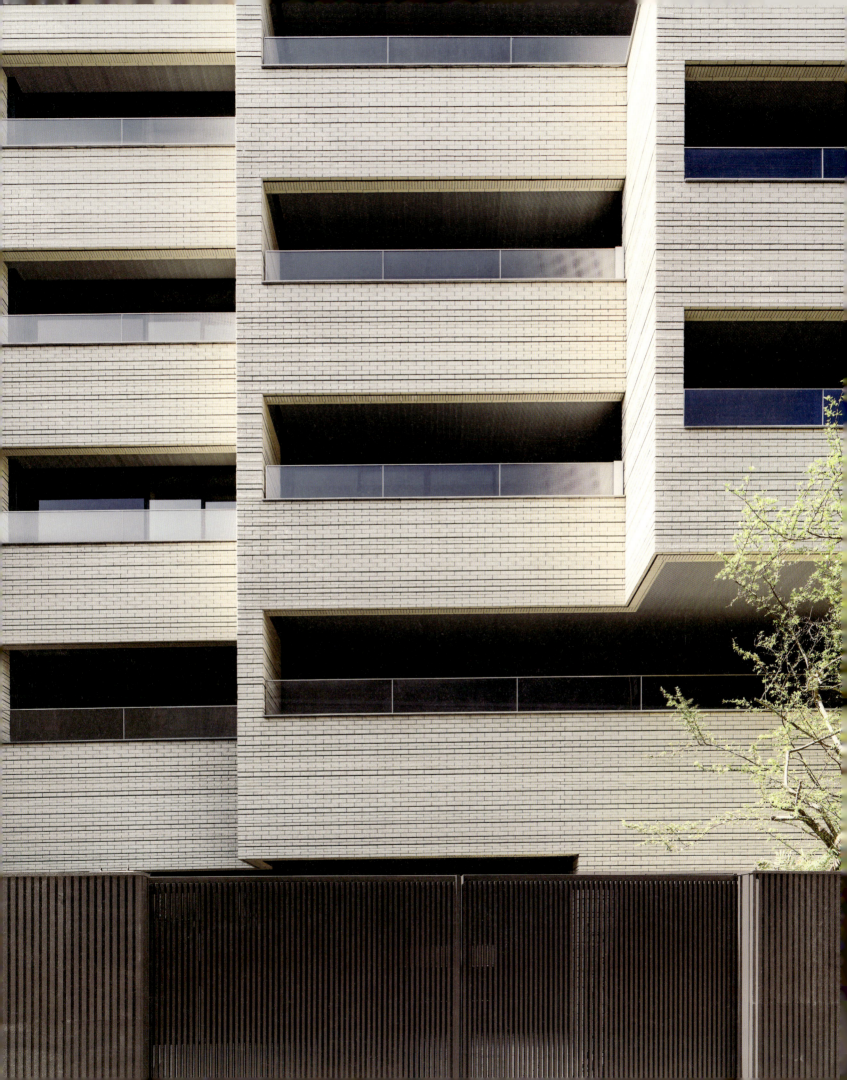

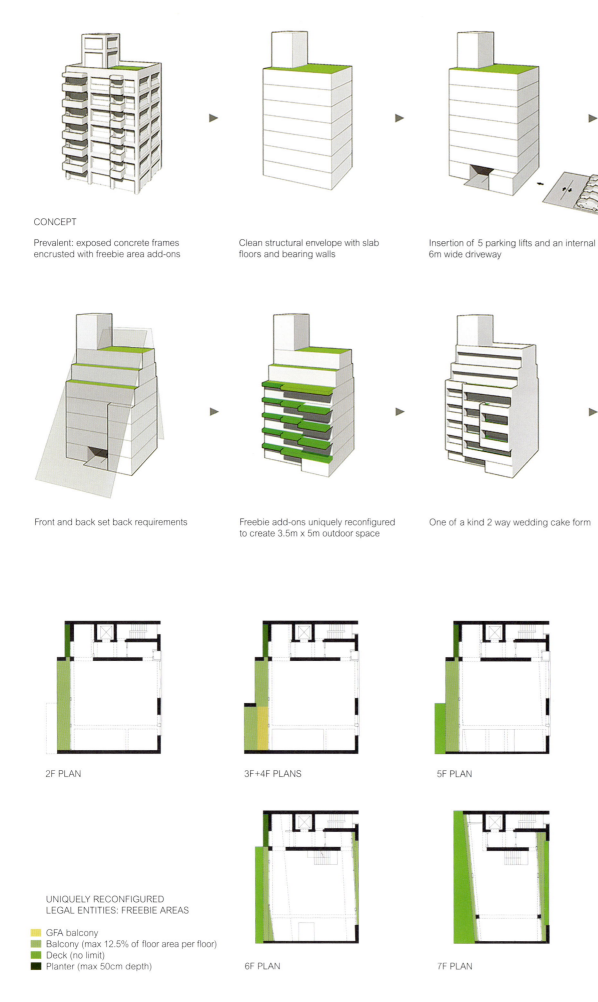

CONCEPT

Prevalent: exposed concrete frames
encrusted with freebie area add-ons

Clean structural envelope with slab
floors and bearing walls

Insertion of 5 parking lifts and an internal
6m wide driveway

Front and back set back requirements

Freebie add-ons uniquely reconfigured
to create 3.5m x 5m outdoor space

One of a kind 2 way wedding cake form

2F PLAN

3F+4F PLANS

5F PLAN

UNIQUELY RECONFIGURED
LEGAL ENTITIES: FREEBIE AREAS

GFA balcony
Balcony (max 12.5% of floor area per floor)
Deck (no limit)
Planter (max 50cm depth)

6F PLAN

7F PLAN

The architecture of **xrange**   Inspired by constraints

Secondly, the design strategy for the freebie area add-ons is to unify them into a single architectural element despite their drastically different size and depth. The 60cm deep flower bed, 200cm deep balcony and 350cm deep terrace are merged into a stepped form in plan that stretches over the entire 17m wide street front of the building. The reconfiguration made possible a 3.5m x 5m outdoor living space, creating a new housing layout previously unseen for dense urban living. In addition, stringent site set backs further dictated these reconfigured add-ons into a staggered section from top to bottom of the building envelope, resulting in a one of a kind, two-way wedding cake housing form in the X and Y-axis.

The creative solution of this urban housing project came from direct design responses to existing urban phenomena and rethinking legal constraints. Through the use of an ad hoc structural hybrid paired with concise geometric strategies, the unique stepped architecture form of the housing project achieves a striking purity, and created unparalleled benefits for both developer and housing occupants.

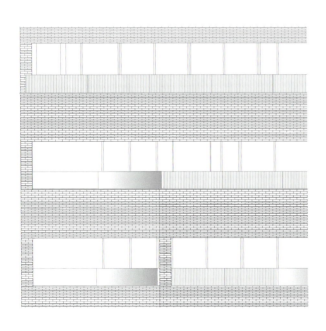

PARTIAL NORTH ELEVATION

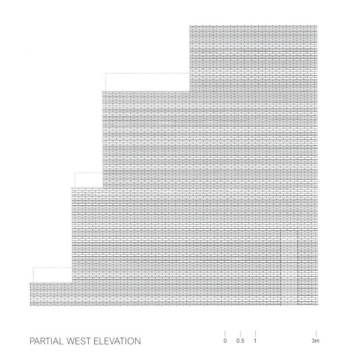

PARTIAL WEST ELEVATION

0	0.5	1	3m

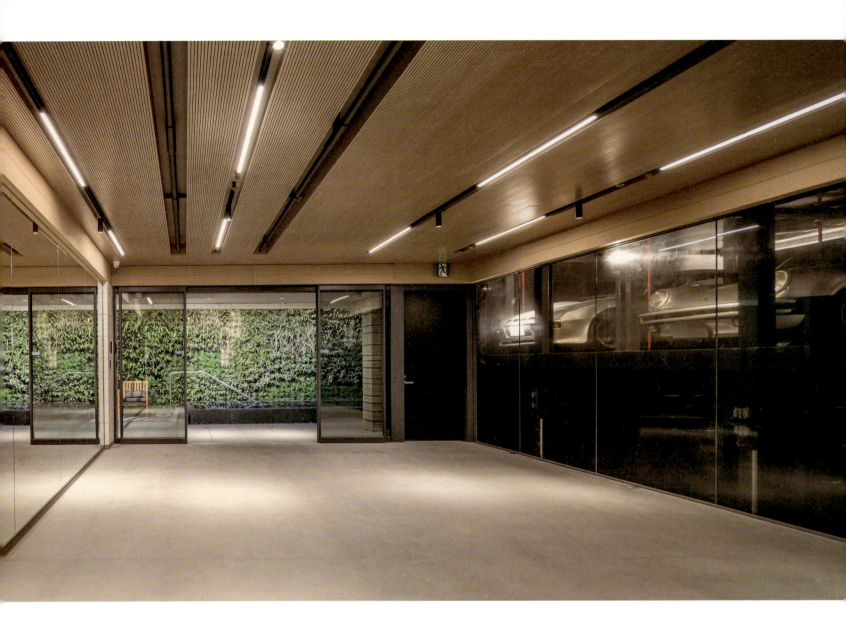

The architecture of **xrange**   Inspired by constraints

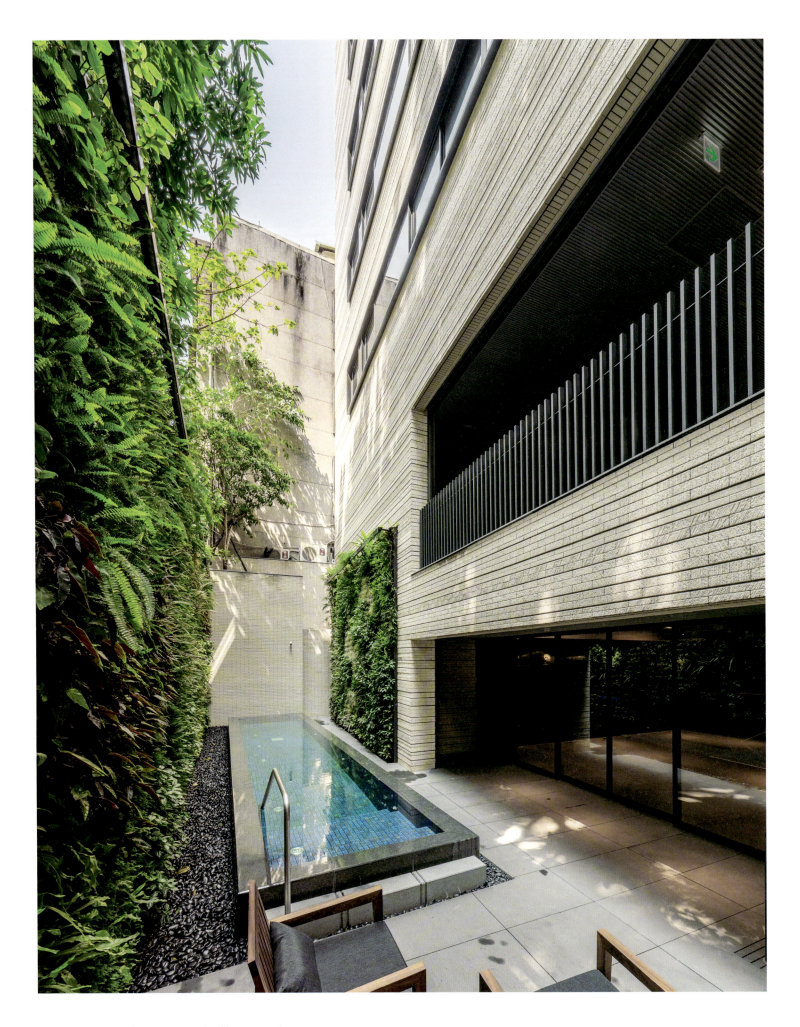

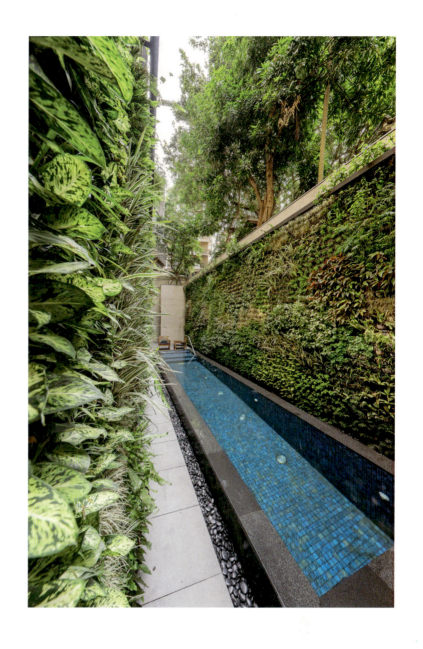

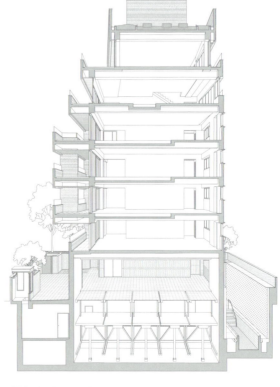

SECTION PERSPECTIVE

The architecture of **xrange**   Inspired by constraints

The Cloud
— An environmentally responsive balloon structure

A beacon for the 2008 Taiwan Designers' Week, the Cloud is a self-floating temporary canopy on the outdoor 44 South Village Civic Plaza where the design fair is held. Having participated in the plaza's design several years back, where the demolished roofscape of the 1948 army quarters was transformed into grounded green slopes on the plaza, the Cloud—descending from above—forms an interesting urban dialog with the site's history.

The Cloud has a body mass of 900m^3 that is buoyed by a 10x30x3m transparent balloon space frame encased in a soft translucent sac of synthetic fibers. The massive balloon space frame is made up of 12 balloons, 3.5m in diameter and filled with 150,000L of helium gas, which are tied into a 3D web structure with the balloons acting as "nodes" and nylon ropes as tensile members. The balloons are positioned at varying heights and are connected from imaginary center to imaginary center with precision engineered ropes of various lengths and angles that are tied onto custom attachments points on the balloons' curved surfaces.

The Cloud defines an outdoor hang out area for events and DJ parties with its shape-shifting mass that responds to wind movements and air pressure changes. Through its soft translucent membrane skin, the Cloud filters scorching sunlight into an ephemeral glow. As air pressure drops before rain falls, the Cloud will react by lowering from its 9 to 12m flying height to hover just above ground, therefore "predicting" rain during the hot summer week.

The Cloud combines CAD/CAM with a very simple design concept: using minimal means and everyday materials to create surprising environmentally responsive effects.

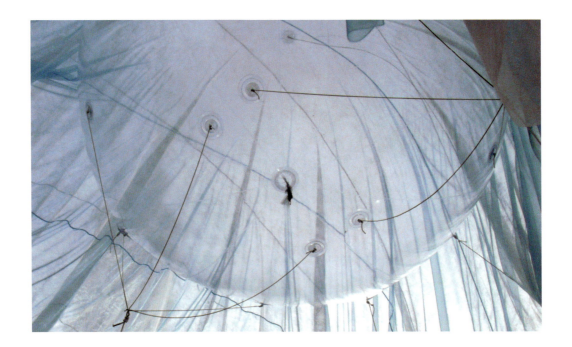

cloud

grass mounds

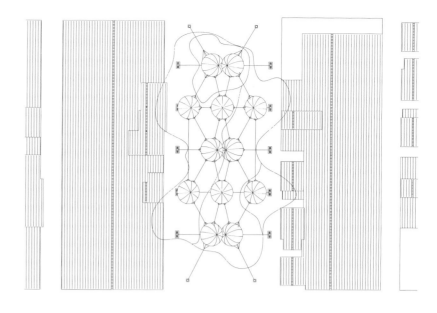

PLAN

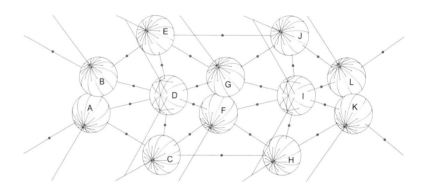

TENSILE SYSTEM - ROPE LENGTH VARIATIONS

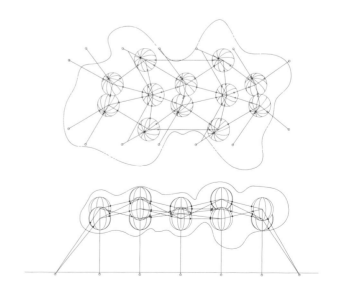

STRUCTURAL DIAGRAM

Winbond Electronics Corporation
— Tower of green pockets

For Winbond Corporation, a total memory solution provider in Taiwan, the Zhubei building is designed to reflect the client's core value of fostering well being for workers, and commitment to ecological preservation and education. The design goal was to provide a green Gold Energy listed (the second highest energy designation in Taiwan), people-centric work space for collaboration and sharing while working within the uniform efficiency of cubicles that accommodates the legions of high tech workers occupying 19 floors of offices.

The concept of Green Pockets as places for physical and mental recharge becomes the driving force for the architecture. Green Pockets are refuge areas of greenery for resting, mingling, brainstorming and informal meetings away from the uniformity and long hours spent at the cubicles. Vertically stacked, these Green Pockets become large scale "flutings" on the tower and form the wavy design of the Tower of Green Pockets.

The form concept produced great environmental benefits upon solar heat gain analysis. Unlike large, flat, south facing curtain wall surface which would get constant direct solar exposure throughout the day, the wavy flutes of the tower create vertical shadow zones that glide across the tower's elevation throughout the day in the exceedingly hot summers. In the winter, the wavy folds become favorable heat traps. The temperature of the curtain wall thus stays cool in the summer and warm in the winter.

The tower houses a dining floor with garden patio, a gym and a yoga studio. On the ground floor, there is a cafe and an exhibition gallery dedicated to environmental awareness and ecological preservation. Extending the architecture concept, wood is used extensively throughout the lobby. The 8m tall main lobby wall is clad in wood panels along its entire 90m length.

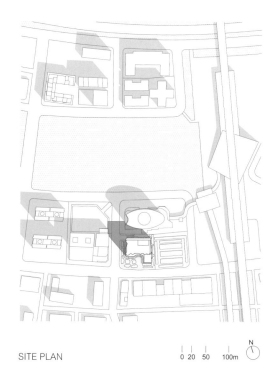

SITE PLAN

0 20 50 100m N

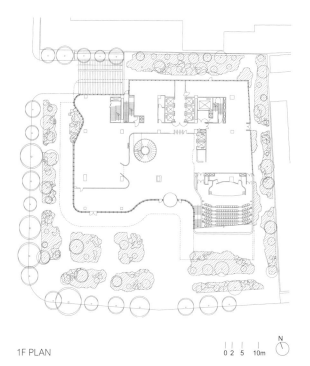

1F PLAN

0 2 5 10m N

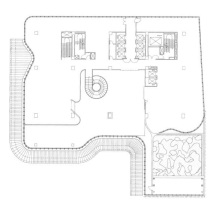

2F PLAN

3F PLAN

A spiral staircase 6.8m in diameter connects the lobby to the meeting rooms on the second floor and the dining hall and garden on the third floor. A unique wood screen design that is created by vertical batons structurally interlocked with wooden blocks becomes the design language for railings and partition screens.

Winbond Electronics Corporation auditorium is the highlight of the public programs. The auditorium juts off the ground floor to create an urban patio underneath. To reflect the client's on-going support of art and culture, the auditorium showcases a unique wooden roof structure, based on the traditional Chinese dougong which is a stacked and cantilevered timber structure. The modernized dougong is crafted from engineered wood, which allows the dougong members to lift and cantilever at a diagonal to form a spacious diamond lattice of modular 8-point stars. The structure is visible from the street through a window wall at the top of the auditorium. The warm wood color on the entire ground floor gives a strong and continuous visual identity from the street.

The architecture of **xrange** Inspired by constraints

10:00 12:00 14:00 16:00

SHADOW ELEVATIONS

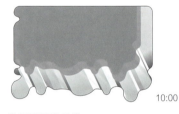  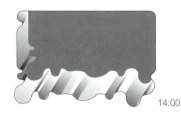 

10:00 12:00 14:00 16:00

SHADOW PLANS

  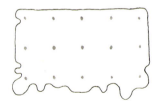 

An office plan with "pocket greenhouses" stacked vertically to become folds on the tower elevation

—— Shadow zone
——▶ Sun angle

CONCEPT

The architecture of **xrange**   Inspired by constraints

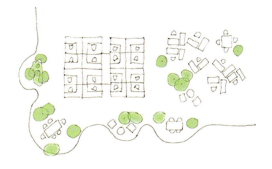

"Pocket greenhouses"

SKETCHES

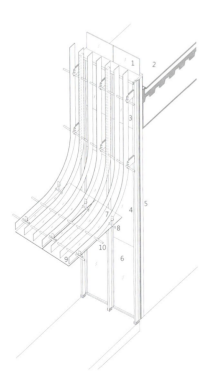

1F FACADE SYSTEM

1. 10+10mm SGP laminated low iron glass railing
2. 3rd floor slab with raise stone flooring
3. 12mm laminated low iron heat strengthened glass with spandrel panel
4. 70x150mm solid core steel wind column
5. 75x225mm curtain wall mullion
6. 12mm laminated low iron heat strengthened curtain wall glass
7. 10+10mm SGP laminated low iron glass canopy
8. Stainless steel spider brackets
9. 16mm steel fin canopy structure
10. 50mm steel rod

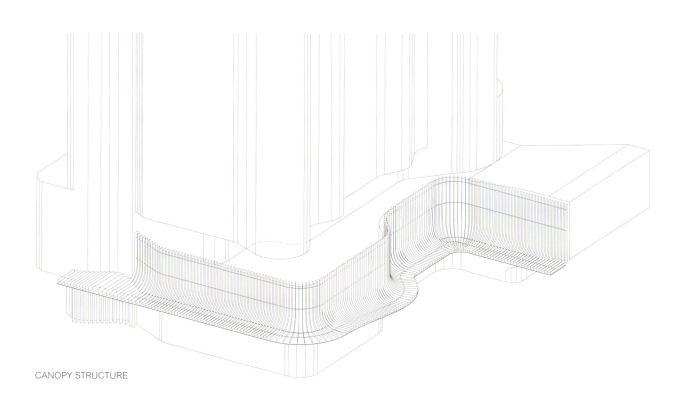

CANOPY STRUCTURE

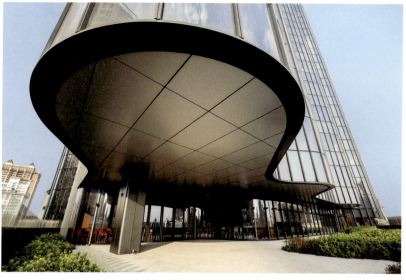

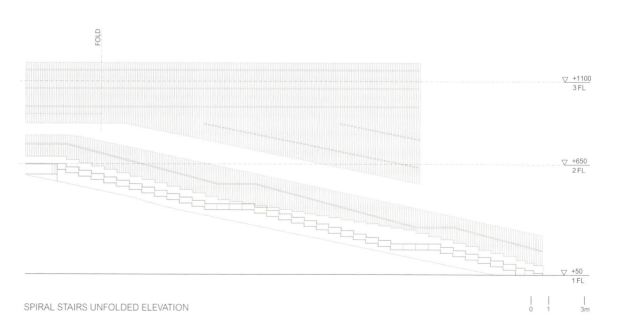

FOLD

▽ +1100
3 FL

▽ +650
2 FL

▽ +50
1 FL

SPIRAL STAIRS UNFOLDED ELEVATION

0   1   3m

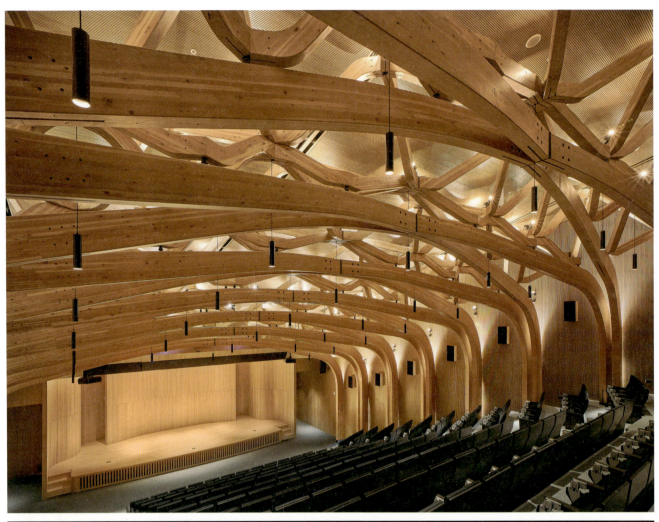

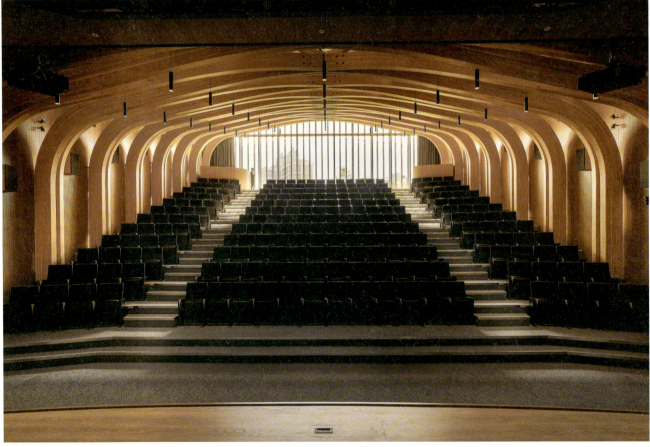

The architecture of **xrange**   Inspired by constraints

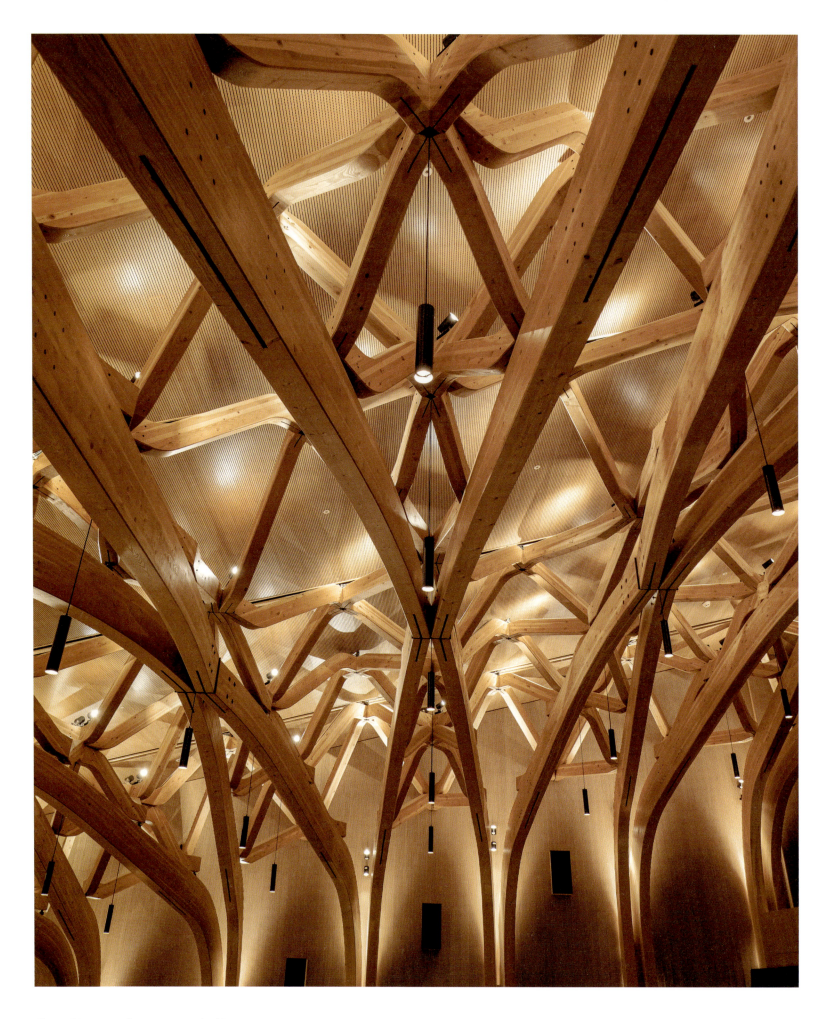

1. Steel structural connector
2. Recessed steel plate connector for douggong
3. Glulam Y-column lower part 1, 16x43~45cm
4. Glulam Y-column part 2, 16x30~43cm
5. 16x160mm steel friction bolts

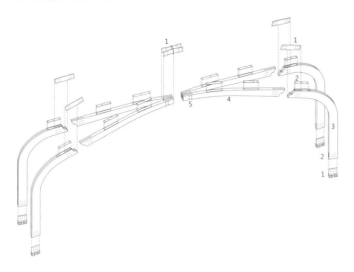

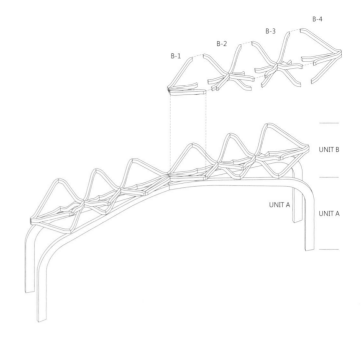

Y BEAM STRUCTURE UNIT A

AUDITORIUM STRUCTURE UNIT

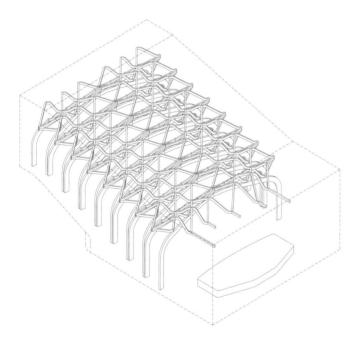

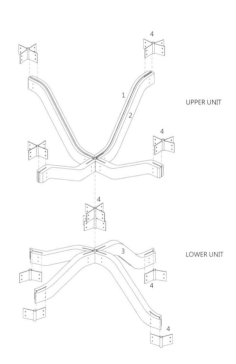

AUDITORIUM STRUCTURE

DOUGGONG STRUCTURAL UNIT B-3

1. Recessed groove for wirings
2. Upper glulam douggong, 12x18cm cross section
3. Lower glulam douggong, 12x18cm cross section
4. Steel structural connector with 16x160mm friction bolts

— LAYERING complexities

These projects are sculpted from the inside out by layering diverse, multiple aspects of space and use. **Ant Farm House** is an ultrathin new abode built above and over an old stone house, preserving the original stone house as the "found interior" for the new house which becomes the "internalized exterior" of the old. **House of Music** is a tower house whose design allows a couple's musical synergy to permeate throughout the house across different floors and during separate activities. Taking layering to a new dimension, **Beetle House** channels the structure of a beetle wherein the house is protected from typhoon, sun and insects by the layering of hard and soft functional skins and freed from room layouts. Finally **HAX** is given a layered, dual personality, with a "dancing" column system that supports 2 beam expressions, one emotional/curved for culture programs and the other utilitarian/rectilinear for industrial programs.

Ant Farm House
— An ultrathin new house built over an old stone house

A new layer of living spaces wraps around an existing indigenous stone house to create a new house of outrageous living proportions, with each "room" averaging about 4m², 80-180cm wide, but with soaring 7m ceiling height. The new house layer holds the entry foyer, study, dog house, library, bathrooms, pantry and service areas that wraps around the stone house in a sequence of small narrow vertical spaces that interlock like the spaces within an ant colony.

The original house was built in the late 1950s with stacked solid granite blocks topped with concrete beams, and is representative of the early houses built in the Yang Ming Shan National Park surrounding protected areas of that period. The design concept sought to preserve the

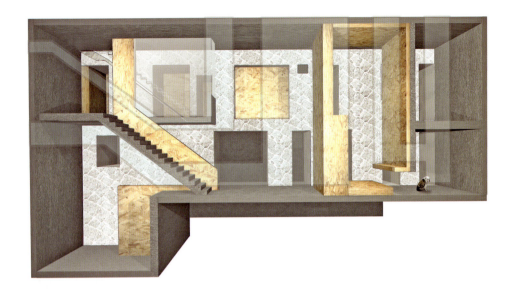

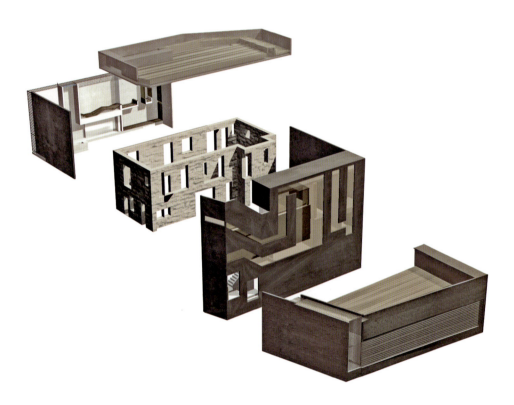

The architecture of **xrange**   Inspired by constraints

original stone house and to improve its seismic performance by adding two steel box-frames onto the front and back of the stone structure to act as lateral structural reinforcement as well as privacy screen layer to the existing house.

This form strategy creates a "found interior" for the new house from the "internalized exterior" of the old stone house. The original windows, doors and air conditioner openings are transformed into exterior/interior windows and doorways or display nooks depending on their location and orientation. Views of surrounding mountains and the city below are revealed through the overlapping of new and old openings, their organic juxtapositions giving a unique quality to the house. The double-layer structure, the house within the house, with the green lawn on its roof also helps with temperature regulation, keeping the stone house warm in winter and cool in summer.

With living spaces intertwined between the old and new structures, the Ant Farm House has a unique spatial texture that transcends typical villas and mansions. The canyon-like master bath has an extreme spatial dimension of 5.5m x 0.8m x 7m in length, width and height. The master shower is suspended above the guest bathroom, with its glass roof overhead creating the feeling of showering outdoors while being sheltered indoors. The kitchen enjoys a two-story light well over the pantry. From the foyer, a pair of 7m high wooden doors open into a 3m² study that is only a desk wide; above is the interior window that opens to the family room on the second floor; while under the desk is the dog house. The three-story entrance foyer and stairway opens to a large and spacious terrace. Within the original stone house on the first floor is an open plan living area, while its second floor houses the family room and three bedrooms, each with its own private ultra-narrow outdoor or indoor light well or terrace.

The Ant Farm House is a multitude of intricate living spaces carved out between the old and the new houses with a simple and uncluttered clarity that is kept understated and raw. The new addition of tall, narrow living spaces over the old stone house resulted in an intimate and modest dwelling without any of the expected convention for luxury.

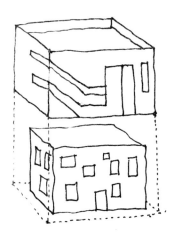
SKETCH

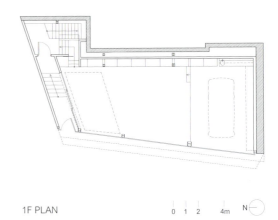

1F PLAN

0 1 2 4m N

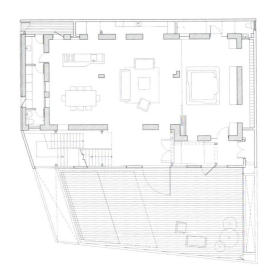

2F PLAN

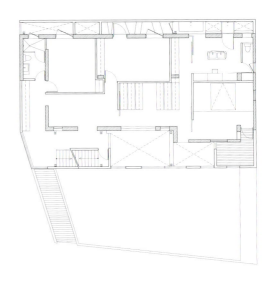

3F PLAN

The architecture of **xrange**   Inspired by constraints

The architecture of **xrange**   Inspired by constraints

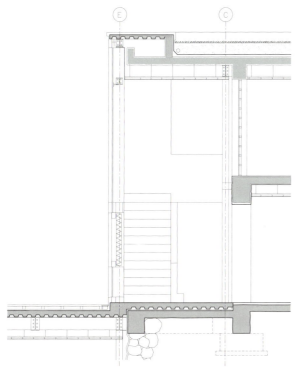

FOYER SECTION

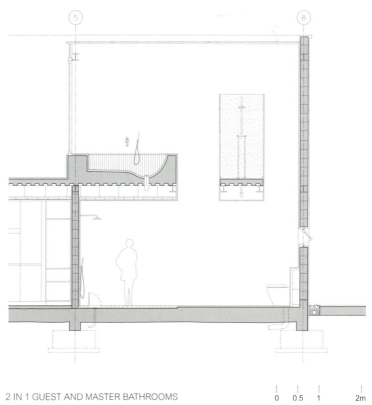

2 IN 1 GUEST AND MASTER BATHROOMS

0   0.5   1   2m

House of Music
— House as musical instrument

Designed for two musicians, a symphony conductor and an award-winning oboist, House of Music is a six-story family home in the Shilin district of Taipei. The design concept places the music room, called the Music Box, as the central organizational element of the house. The Music Box is a place for making music, whereas the concrete tower structure of the house becomes a "reverberation chamber," allowing the couple's musical synergy to float throughout the house across different floors and during separate activities. The design concept expresses the clients' belief that the act of music should not be hidden behind sound proofed doors but should be immersive into everyday living activities. The house thus becomes a spatial musical instrument, where one can appreciate music in any corner of the house, whether cooking, eating, sitting or sleeping.

The Music Box on the third floor sits in the middle of the five story house, a vertical sound and light channel that links the living areas below and the bedrooms above, and has auditorium-style seating to accommodate both formal recitals and impromptu gatherings. The Music Box is built from 400 walnut angled panels, 150 of which are operable, forming a porous screen system to the living areas, bedrooms and bathrooms. Sections of this screen system can be opened or closed independently, thereby allowing sounds from the Music Box to be "tuned" in and out depending on spatial use and occasion. The exterior design is inspired by musical notations, with windows dancing like black notes on the horizontal line patterns cast into the concrete. The windows defy the convention of following the sizes and functions of the spaces behind, they are intentionally non-hierarchical and are placed to express rhythm and musicality on the building exterior. Throughout the interior, the use of brass, cork and other materials commonly found in musical instruments further enhances the concept of the house as a musical instrument. The wine cellar in the basement with a generous capacity of 1,500 bottles is inspired by red wine swirling freely in a glass, its organic form in bold purple marry the client's favorite color with his passion for wine.

The House of Music tells the musicians' story from the inside out, a story that connects their past, their work, their hobbies, their family, and their future.

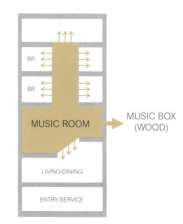

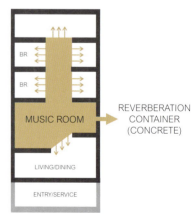

DIAGRAMS

The architecture of **xrange**   Inspired by constraints

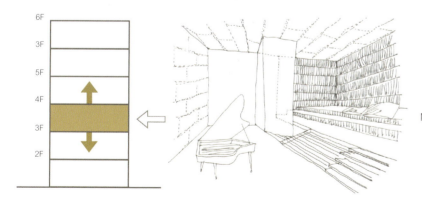

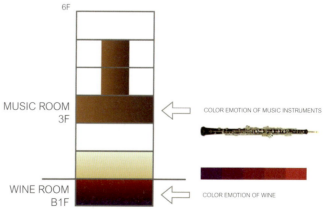

MUSIC ROOM
3F

COLOR EMOTION OF MUSIC INSTRUMENTS

WINE ROOM
B1F

COLOR EMOTION OF WINE

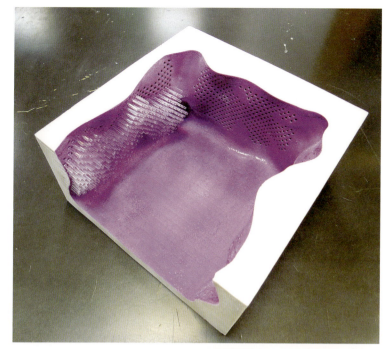

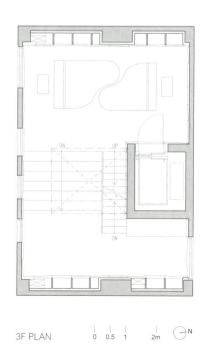

3F PLAN   0 0.5 1   2m   N

— LAYERING complexities

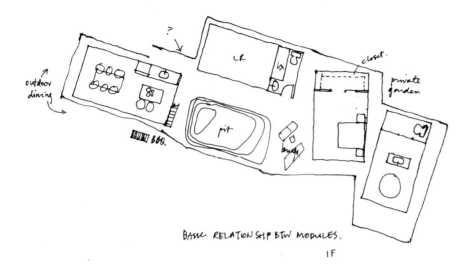

SKETCH

Beetle House
— Hard shell with soft membrane protects a house that is 80% semi-outdoor

On the Pacific coast of eastern Taiwan, verdant subtropical Taitung county is also the very place where strong summer typhoons often make landfall. The Beetle House is a weekend home for an insect-phobic homeowner to enjoy the outdoor life of Taitung's Dulan region without the threat of typhoons or insects. Driven by the aspect of protection, the Beetle House observes the structure of a beetle whereby a hard outer shell protects the soft membrane wings and inner body underneath, the two parts unfolding separately when flying, and folding back into one upon landing. This integrated yet distinct functionality of the beetle's shell and wings inspired the design of the house.

The Beetle House is made up of a semi-outdoor rigid fiberglass cage, underneath which is a soft inner shell of insect netting and sun shading. This outermost layer of the house has shutters that can be completely closed in the event of a typhoon to protect the living functions within it,

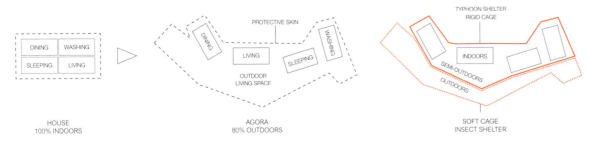

DIAGRAM

The architecture of **xrange** Inspired by constraints

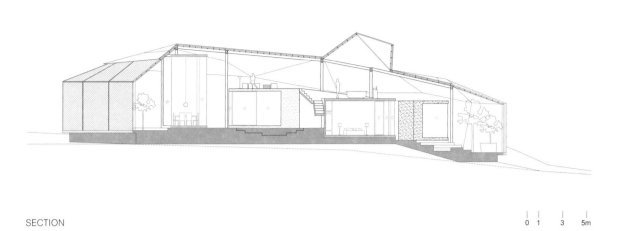

SECTION

0 1   3   5m

and to prevent the inner layer of solar shading and insect nettings from being damaged by branches and detritus brought by typhoons.

The hard and soft double-layer structure thus forms the building envelope and its spatial organization. Within the envelope, the living room, kitchen/dining room, bedroom and bathroom are designed as four prefabricated weather-tight boxes laid out organically in plan, while the remaining 75% floor area of the 300m^2 house becomes semi-outdoor spaces to take advantage of the pleasant climate of Taitung. To minimize the building's impact on site, each prefab box structure measures 3x6m for ease of transport to site and has independent air conditioning systems, while the semi-outdoor spaces rely on natural ventilation to achieve effective temperature control.

The house expands towards the Pacific Ocean for vast sea views, the undulating roof lines echoing the Dulan mountains behind. At night, the translucent fiberglass cage and inner shell of nettings turn the house into a soft, glowing sculpture.

The Beetle House takes cues from the natural environment of Taitung and reinterprets the idea of a green building as a unique and organic architecture integrated with the land.

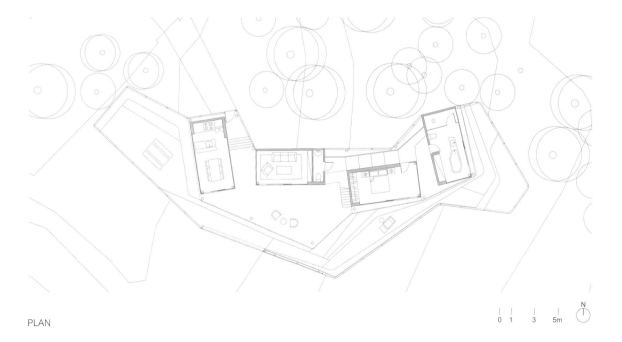

PLAN

0 1   3   5m   N

The architecture of **xrange**   Inspired by constraints

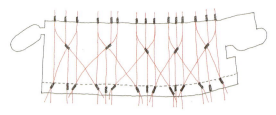

"Dancing" structure grid: column grid with 2 distinct beam systems

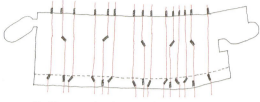

Bent beam system 1

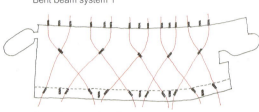

DANCING STRUCTURE CONCEPT   Curve beam system 2

HAX
— Dancing structure with 2 beam systems

Located in an industrial zone of a Taipei suburb, HAX is conceived as the headquarters of the Hong Foundation (HAX = Hong; Art/Architecture/Automobile; Experimentation). The Hong Foundation was founded over 50 years ago, its five decades of support to education and culture is a legacy that is synonymous with the social and cultural heritage of Taiwan. Now moving forward with new leadership, the foundation aims to expand its programs and reach, and build an "everything" headquarters of sorts. Intended as a place for culture, exhibition, and collection while on the other hand functioning as offices, development studios and workshops, HAX is simultaneously a cultural/arts building and a workshop/industrial building.

This dual role drove the design to explore the fusing of opposites, to rethink if the industrial building typology, typically medium height concrete construction with banded windows, can be elevated to the emotional. The building thus has a dual personality: a melding of creative/emotional and utility/rational qualities.

In plan, the "dancing columns" system engage in a playful stance, instead of being dictated by constraints such as a parking grid underneath. The columns stand at various angles and positions to support 2 distinct beam systems, a "kinked" linear system and an "x" curvy system for different floors depending on the program.

The building overlooks the Guandu "flatlands"—an enormous expanse of green space under ecological protection. A river on the site's front edge runs from the central mountain range of Taipei on its right to the Tamsui River estuary to its left. On this elevation, the building's façade, rendered in concrete and glass, takes on a liquid, wavy appearance that transitions to a horizontal, linear one. The building's ground floor entry is located at the point at which the façade changes its personality.

HAX challenges the norm of Taiwanese industrial buildings with a design that reflects and celebrates the client's legacy and the activity taking place within. From the flatlands, HAX seemingly undergoes a metamorphosis as it absorbs the organic energy waves of its natural context to transfigure to its orthogonal, industrial context. It is a final effect of acceleration, speed and movement, metaphors befitting the ambition of the client.

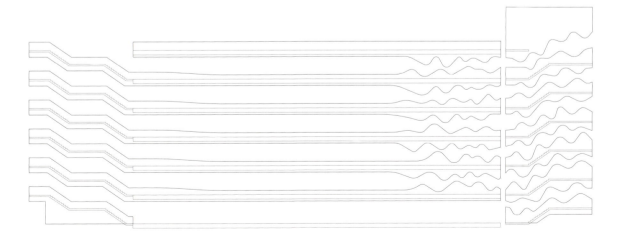

ELEVATION CONCEPT

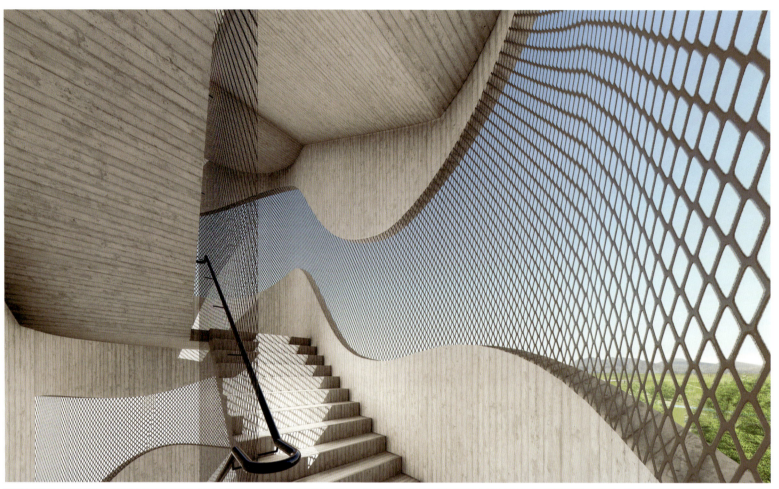

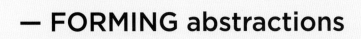

— FORMING abstractions

Transforming their contexts into unique sculptural forms, these projects seek to synthesize an idea into a story that reflects the essence and aspiration of their architectural formation. **Stone Cloud** plays on the weightiness and permanence of stone versus the lightness and ephemeral nature of clouds in a cemetery. **Penghu House** abstracted the site's historical and cultural heritage dating to the Qing dynasty into a village cluster form with a distinctive roof profile above fields and trees. **Sea Rock** echoes adjacent basalt cliffs, but redefine them into a tapestry of local colors and textures. **Urban Scope** celebrates the site's rapid pace of urban development with a "skyline" structure. **Petals** expresses the client's plum confectionary business with curved forms inspired by fruit blossoms. **Landscape of Traces** interprets 130 years of urban transformations on the site of Taiwan's first railway as historical imprints or urban traces to be abstractly revealed to the public.

Stone Cloud

On a hill top with views of the Tamsui River, a shelter reimagines the fusion of 2 elements that are antithetical in matter and spirit: stone and cloud. Weight and mass are used in striking contrast against lightness and the ephemeral. Stone is expressed as shading, a layer of light and shadows suspended above like a cloud. The stones' variegated matte and polished surfaces reflect the sky conditions as a moving pattern of shadows overhead.

The architecture of **xrange**   Inspired by constraints

Penghu House
— A modern house inspired by the indigenous coral stone houses of Penghu

On the Penghu archipelago west of Taiwan, indigenous laogushi or coral stone houses are a unique cultural heritage. With roots in the southern Chinese coastal regions of the Qing dynasty, coral stone houses were built of actual coral blocks stacked upon a base wall of basalt quarried on the islands. They are characterized by a nine-square plan, distinctive "rolled" roof ridges resembling a curved gable and "slits and pillars" as window openings due to strong winds. The design for the multi-generation Penghu family is inspired by these historical coral house clusters on windswept plains of wild chrysanthemum.

Consisting of three parallel stacked volumes, each with a distinctive roof profile, the Penghu house evokes an indigenous village cluster above the tree lines. The traditional slits-and-pillars openings are reinterpreted as balcony and patio screens, behind which are floor to ceiling

glass doors for greatly improved natural lighting and ventilation. The white stone cladding casts a strong contrast against the azure island sky and the surrounding green farmland.

The three living volumes form the parti of the house as well as the structural system of load bearing walls. The central block houses the 5m tall living room or grand hall for family gatherings and festivals. The east volume next to it is a courtyard that connects the parents' bedrooms and the ancestral temple upstairs. The kitchen and dining is in the west volume and on the top floor, the master bedroom opens onto the roofscape of rolled ridges with sweeping views of the sea. On this level, the 3 roof silhouettes interconnect; the roof deck, pitch and ridges flow to create a rolling, continuous spatial experience.

As part of the climate strategies, there are minimal window openings to the northeast due to severe winter winds, while deep overhangs and slit-and-pillar patio screens are placed on the south and west faces to reduce direct solar exposure. The roofscape and exterior walls are 30cm thick and fully clad in rain screen granite panel system, giving the house extra insulation to withstand the summer heat and gale-force winds in the winter. Within the compound is a natural wellspring and a small organic farming patch for the family.

Effective natural cross-ventilation is built-in throughout the entire house, even within the mechanical and duct conduits. This allows the house to enjoy natural breezes without the use of air conditioners even when it is 35°C outside. The bedroom walls are rendered in natural clay to regulate humidity and prevent mold or fungal growth which is common on the island. Within, the rolling roofscape is lined with fragrant pine, giving the house a warm visual and olfactory signature. Wood cut-offs are also recycled into original furniture and screen for the house.

The Penghu House integrates traditional wisdom within a modern framework to create a multi-generational home for a local clan, resulting in a distinctive architecture born from the unique conditions of Penghu.

SKETCH

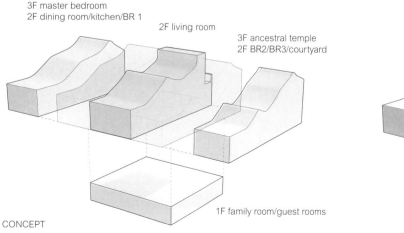

3F master bedroom
2F dining room/kitchen/BR 1

2F living room

3F ancestral temple
2F BR2/BR3/courtyard

1F family room/guest rooms

CONCEPT

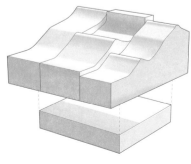

The architecture of **xrange**   Inspired by constraints

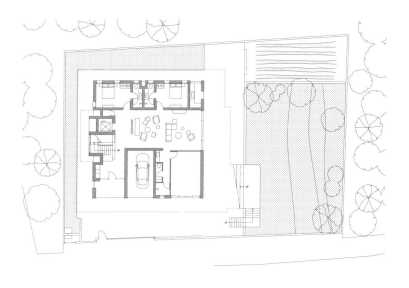

1F PLAN

0 1 3 5m N

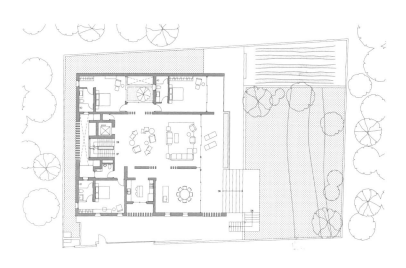

2F PLAN

3F PLAN

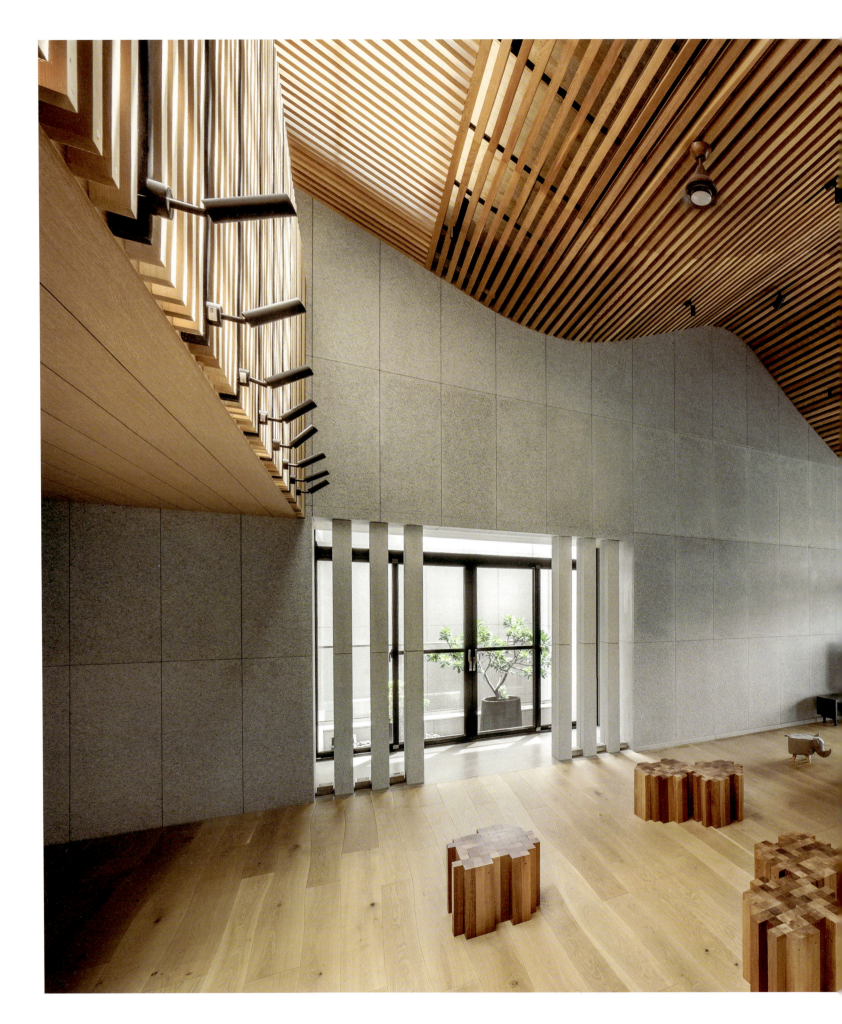

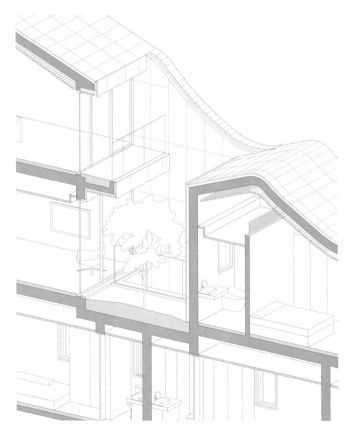

3D COURTYARD SECTION

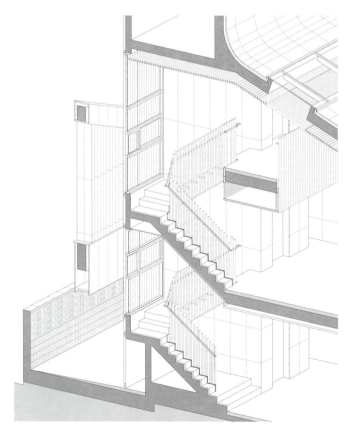

3D STAIR SECTION

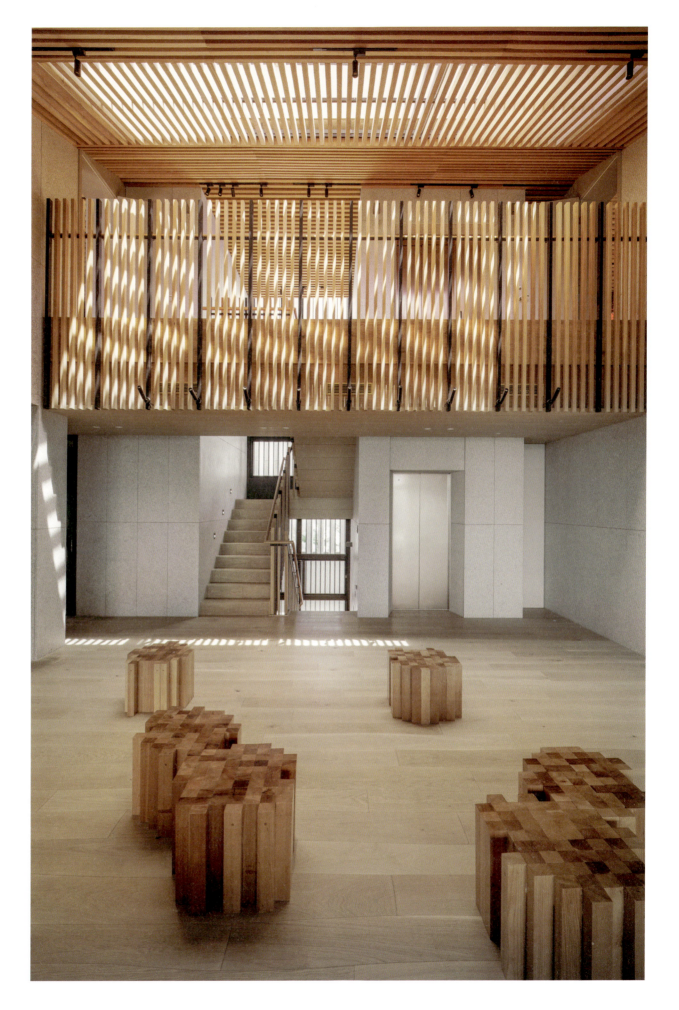

The architecture of **xrange**   Inspired by constraints

Sea Rock
— Craggy forms in local textures

The Sea Rock Hotel is located at the southernmost point of the Penghu archipelago, over-looking the Strait of Taiwan. At the tip of the isolated peninsular land mass, the site enjoys 270 degrees of ocean view. The existing natural condition includes a craggy coastline defined by basalt pillars as well as waters well known for their coral reefs—making it a popular desti-nation for divers, with diving access points and scenic formations accessible on foot minutes away from the hotel. The site's native landscape of dry, desert-like vegetation flourishing among rocky shores is characteristic of Penghu islands due to severe winter winds.

The development comprises a low-slung curved building and a cluster of adjacent villas, their geometry and forms inspired by basalt cliffs that lined the archipelago's coastlines. The main building houses 30 rooms organized in vertical, variegated blocks facing the ocean on the southwestern side. Each room enjoys a balcony and the building is sited to maximize views of the water and the rocky coastline. By reimagining Penghu elements like perforated cement "floral" bricks and colorful glazed bricks in different configurations as balcony screens, the façade of the main building takes on a striated look that recalls the appearance of basalt pillars, rendered in colorful local textures.

On the northeastern, windward side of the main building, walkways are punctuated by a playful stair organization that create a leisurely and organic path to the rooms; their irreg-ularity encourages exploratory or unexpected encounters with cactus gardens, views and other guests from multiple and serendipitous angles.

The villa enclave's high faceted walls echo the island's craggy shoreline. The high walls are a response to the need for privacy and essential wind barriers on the exposed site. Inside the

villas, stone pillars that are stairs lead up to the roof top hang out area with a pool. Under the pillars is the seemingly "excavated" bathtub, raw and rustic against the cactus garden in the protected courtyard outside.

Still in the permit application phase and under development, Sea Rock is envisioned to be run by a luxury hotel company. Hotel facilities include a pool with an adjacent earth mound bar with surrounding sandpits for play—other amenities will be determined as the property's realization nears. In the meantime, the Sea Rock celebrates its isolated, seaside ambience and close proximity to a famed formation of waterside basalt pillars.

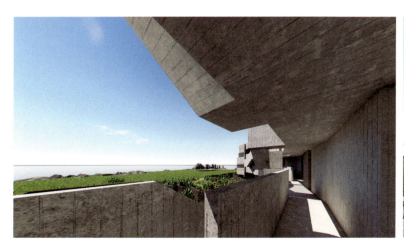

The architecture of **xrange**   Inspired by constraints

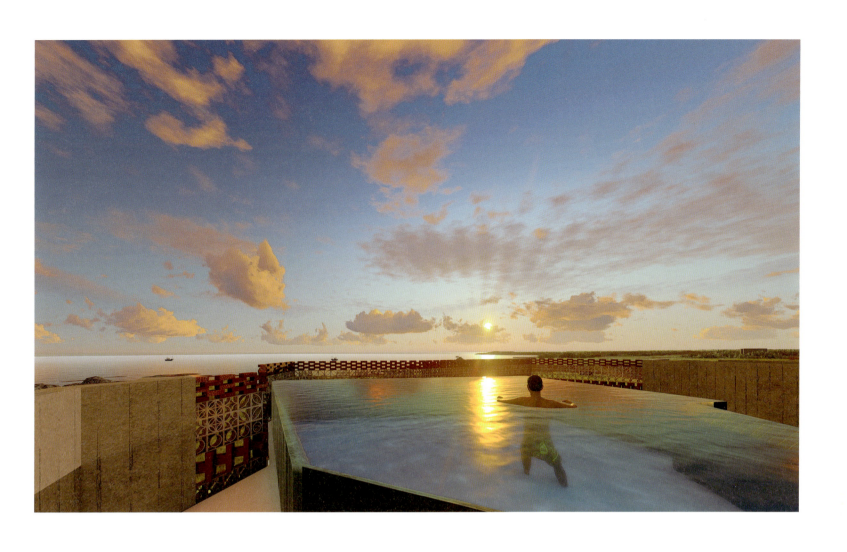

Urban Scope
— Skyline as structure: A telescopic Urban Theater

Urban Scope is located at the historical site of Huashan Station, which was once the largest transportation hub and freight center in Taipei City in the early days. Today, it is a green space adjoining the Huashan 1914 Creative Park and is part of the government's ambitious east to west gateway urban renewal masterplan. The Bureau of Urban Renewal is charged with the creation of this semi-permanent public arts space to reinforce Taipei's vision as a design capital. Straddling the 140m long historical rail platform, Urban Scope intends to reinstate the site's history as a city on the move, an "urban mass" that slides on recycled railway tracks and train wheels to create multiple spatial configurations for various types and scales of events. Urban Scope is a multi-functional public space that can be "transformed," a dynamic pavilion reflecting the dramatic urban transformations of Taipei City.

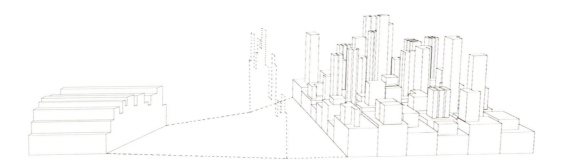

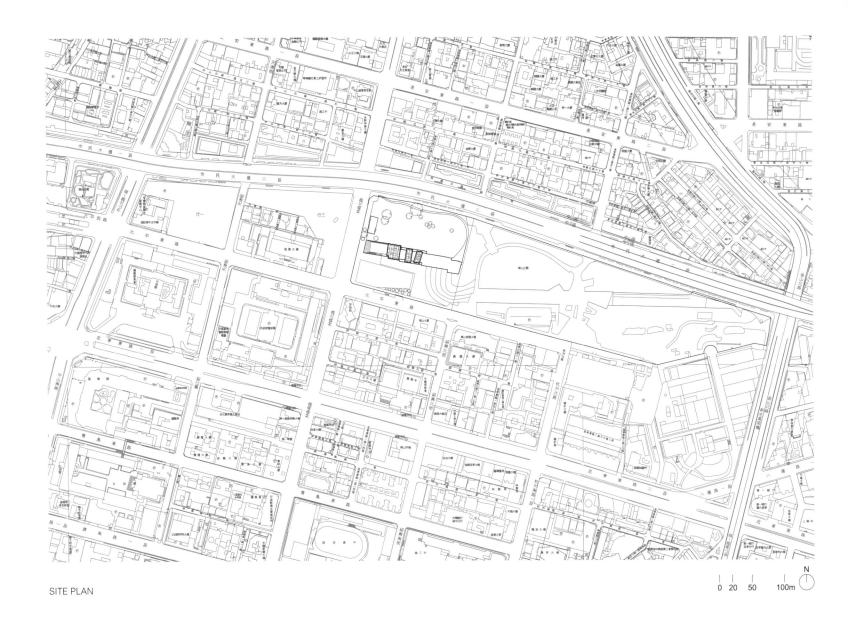

SITE PLAN

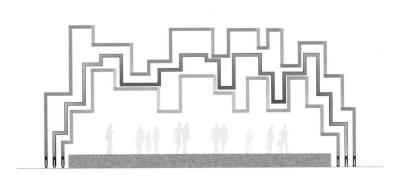

CONCEPT DIAGRAM

The architecture of **xrange**   Inspired by constraints

Framing a telescopic east-west view channel of the city, Urban Scope is inspired by Taipei's city skyline visible from this large open site in the heart of the city. Urban Scope is made up of 7 variations of the "skyline arch," a zigzag structure with a 22m span over the historical railway station platform. Simple repetitions of the skyline arches resulted in a mass that is highly ordered yet organic in expression. The resultant mass evokes the speed and fluid energies of Asian cities. On this site where old meets new, Urban Scope becomes an instrument for observing the pulse of the city.

Reclaimed train tracks and wheels are laid on the sides of the historical platform to become tracks for Urban Scope to glide on. Urban Scope can contract or expand from 30m to 80m long to accommodate events of all types. The structure is surfaced with translucent raw fiberglass panels and industrial netting woven in a zigzag pattern, naturally lit and ventilated. The historical timeline of Huashan Station is etched onto the platform so visitors can walk through the history of the site as they enjoy the events. At night, the structure becomes a luminous body that echoes the city skyline in the distance.

Urban Scope, a telescopic urban theater on the historical platform of Huashan Station, takes the city skyline and transforms it into a new dynamic urban experience of Taipei.

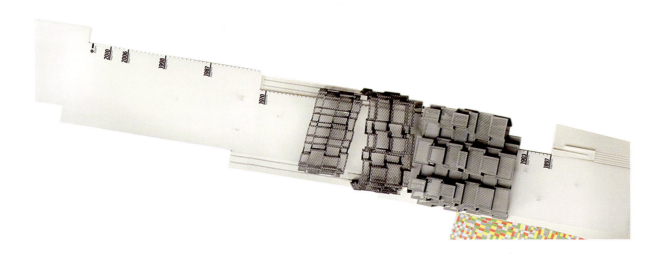

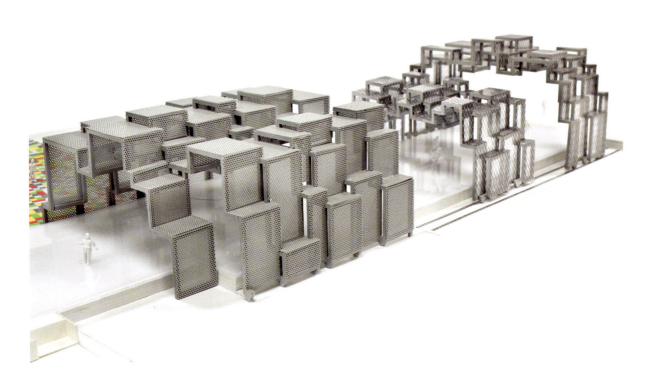

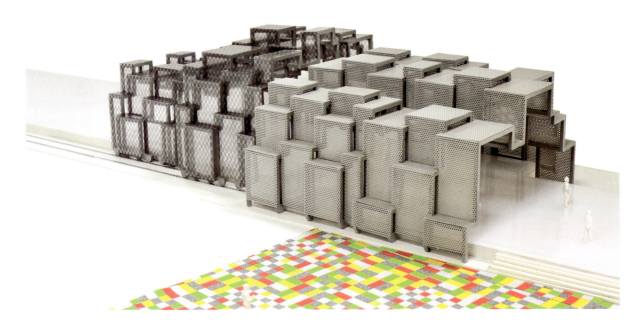

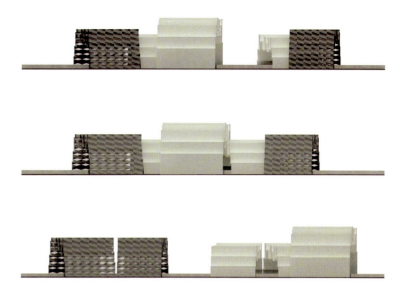

ASSEMBLY 1

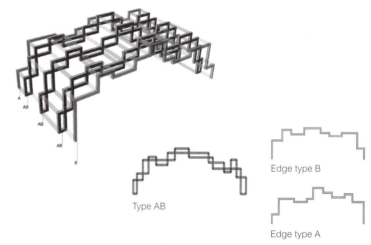

Type AB

Edge type B

Edge type A

SKYLINE STRUCTURE

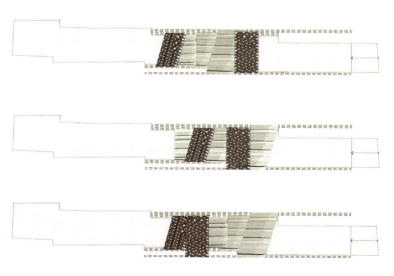

ASSEMBLY 2

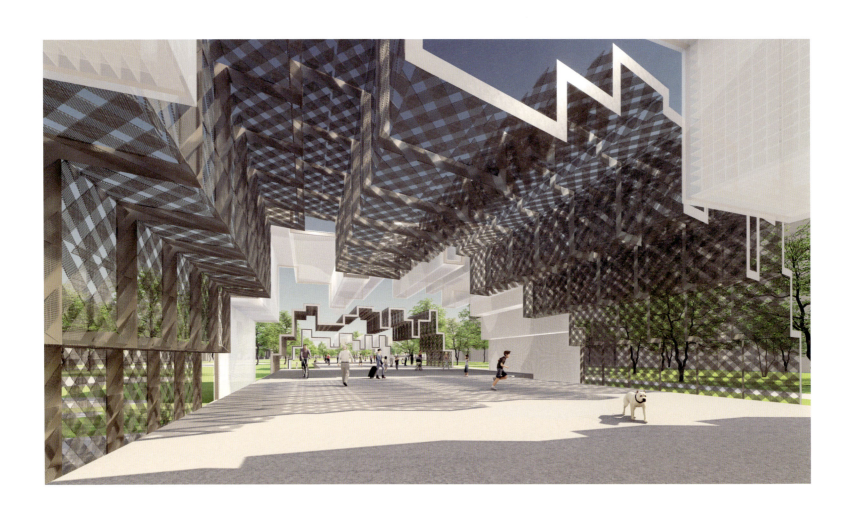

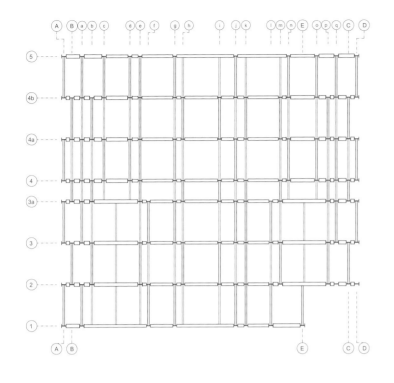

UNIT STRUCTURE PLAN

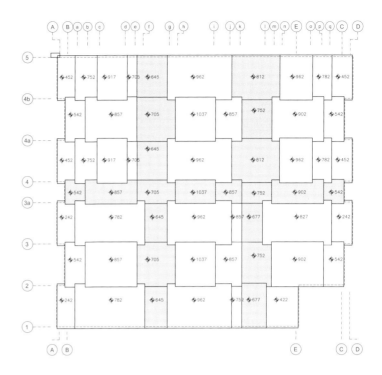

UNIT ROOF PLAN

0 1 3 5m

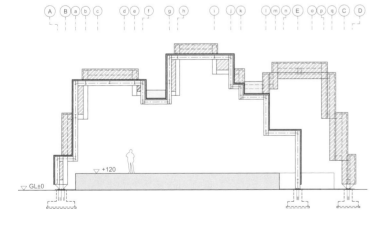

UNIT SECTION A

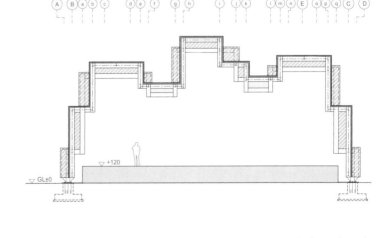

UNIT SECTION B

0 1 3 5m

Petals
— Visitor center inspired by plum blossom petals

Traditional food and agricultural industries under the inevitable pressure to modernize are consistently driven to strengthen their brand identity and cultivate more public awareness to their age old crafts and the culture they reflect. Generally, whole or portions of factory buildings would be converted into a "visiting factory" for visitors to experience the manufacturing processes and enjoy the products in a curated manner. For a traditional savory plum confection maker, their visiting factory will be a showcase and an education center where the confections' manufacturing process from harvesting, sun-drying, seasoning and packaging can be opened to the public through a "factory" tour of sorts. In addition to the two existing buildings for light processing on site, this new "visiting factory" park masterplan includes green houses, kumquat nurseries, a plum orchard, an outdoor market, an administration building and a visitor center.

The design of the visitor center takes inspiration from the factory buildings that are commonly transformed for this purpose. These are typically steel frame structures of 10-15m spans with metal roofs, corrugated metal cladding or concrete block walls. By rethinking this construction expression for these ubiquitous factory sheds, Petals intends to give the visiting factory a new and unique identity.

The visitor center is made up of five oval shaped pavilions, each with its own program and size corresponding to its use and occupancy. Their oval petal roof forms reference plum blossom petals, a nod to the confection brand's origin and specialty. The petal roofs are upturned ovals cantilevered over the steel structure, overlapping each other

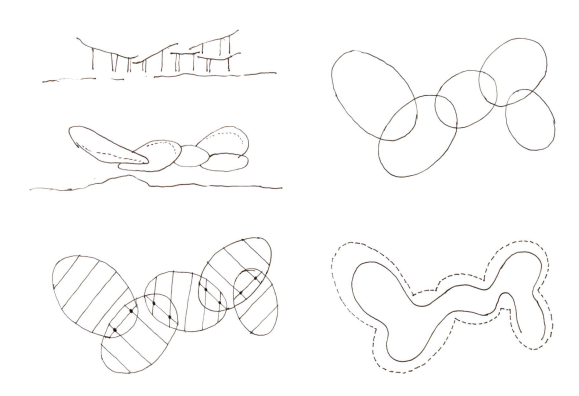

CONCEPT

The architecture of **xrange**   Inspired by constraints

at different heights and orientations. The walls below are horizontally banded concrete blocks with large glass clerestory windows on top. The solid masonry walls ground the buildings, blocking off views of the street while forming soft enclosures to welcome visitors. Overhead, the petal pavilions' overlapping roofs float above the upper glass clerestories to create airy, light filled spaces throughout.

Visitors enter through the lowest petal pavilion. On its left is the largest and tallest petal pavilion which houses shops and cafes in a large open space for visitors to experience the savory confections while enjoying views of the open landscape in front. To the right of the entry petal pavilion, two smaller adjoining pavilions house the brand exhibition area and the conference center. These are multifunctional areas for both local visitors and foreign clientele to understand the confectioner's brand story through exhibition and presentations. From here, visitors enter into an open air petal pavilion which is connected to the administration building and the market square outside.

The administration building houses a convenience store on the ground floor, and offices, classrooms and a bed and breakfast on its upper floors. The market square is lined with a series of curvilinear bamboo canopies for shading. Their curved petal forms are inspired by fruit blossoms, their organic, tree-like formation not only showcases local bamboo crafts, but also becomes a main draw for visitors for the produce and products from small artisanal farms in the surrounding areas.

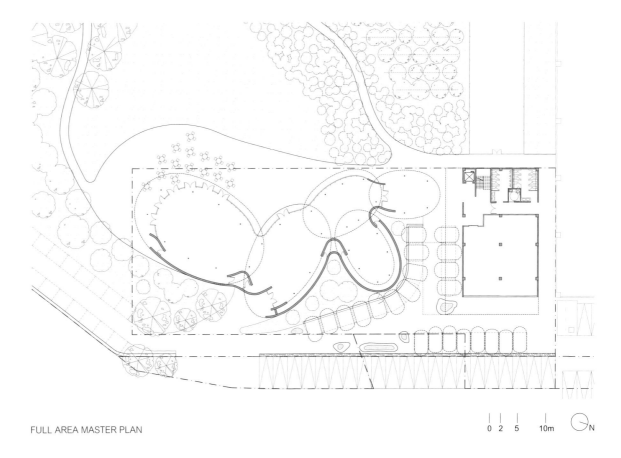

FULL AREA MASTER PLAN

0 2 5 10m N

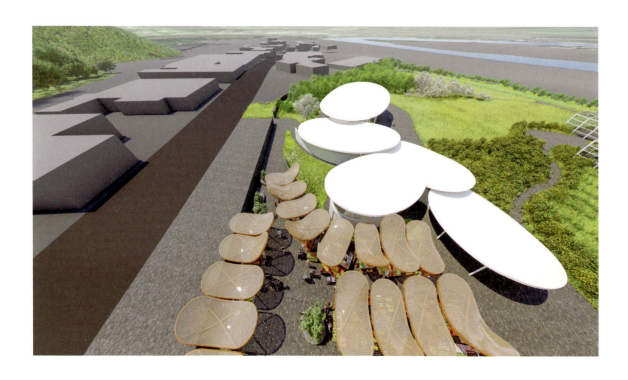

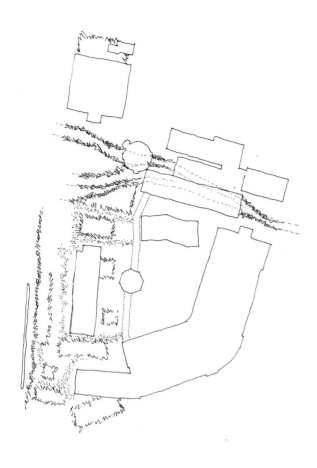

Landscape of Traces
— A century of transformations

The Railway Department Park, part of the National Taiwan Museum, occupies a site that carries 130 years of Taiwan's urban transformation. The first railway of Taiwan originated here during the Qing Dynasty to service the Machinery Bureau which manufactured weapons. It later become the Taipei Artillery Factory and finally the Taipei Railway Factory in 1900. The site sits adjacent to modern day Taipei Main Station, the transportation hub for both the city and northern Taiwan. Designated a national historical monument, the museum park is one of the green focal points in the ambitious Taipei West District Gateway Project, an urban renewal masterplan that stretches across almost a third of downtown Taipei.

Over the past century, there had been many "versions" of the site, survived only by rudimentary maps and records. An industrial service site, constructions on the compound were mostly done by the Japanese in utilitarian and haphazard ways. Buildings were organically packed together and very roughly aligned. Some buildings were even attached directly onto the Qing Dynasty compound walls, cutting windows directly out of the 60 cm thick rubble wall. As the railway hub for over a century, the Railway Department Park's insouciant past of politics, war, industry and urban growth is what draws historians, rail fanatics, and citizens to its storied ground.

The "Landscape of Traces" design concept envisions past transformations on the site as historical imprints or urban traces to be revealed to the public. Archaeological reconstruction was meaningless and impossible as part or most historical remains had already been permanently dug up to make way for train tunnels under the site. In addition, there exists no precise information from which to reconstruct.

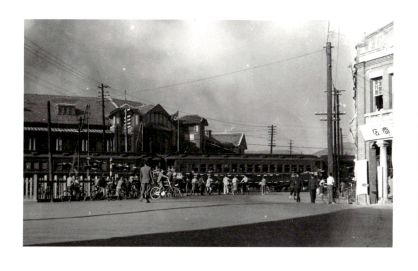

The "blurred," "gradient fade" and "fuzzy edges" landscape design language becomes a strategy for approximations as far as they were known without claiming absolute positions. Traces of past buildings, structures and railway tracks are represented as blurry, lo-fi imprints on the museum grounds, their overlaps and collisions tell the stories of over a century of growth and transformation here.

1885-1895 Machinery bureau, Qing Dynasty

1934 Relocation of railway workshop

1900 Taipei railway workshop

1966 Opening of Tacheng street

1909 Workshop expansion

1982 Opening of Zhongxiao bridge

1918 Railway department office

1991 Widening of civic boulevard

2020 Landscape of Traces

HISTORICAL PLANS

The architecture of **xrange**   Inspired by constraints

SITE PLAN

The architecture of **xrange**   Inspired by constraints

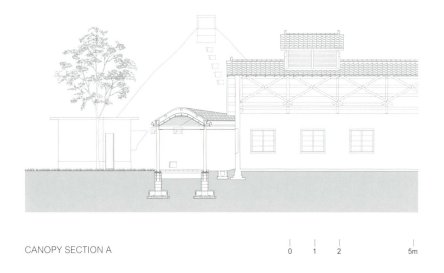

CANOPY SECTION A

0　1　2　　　5m

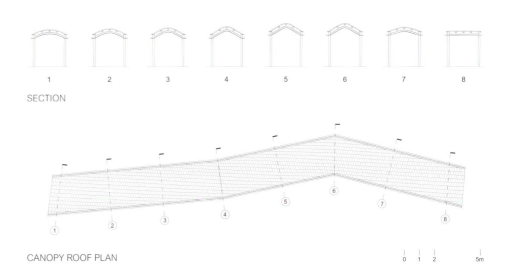

1 2 3 4 5 6 7 8

SECTION

CANOPY ROOF PLAN

0 1 2   5m

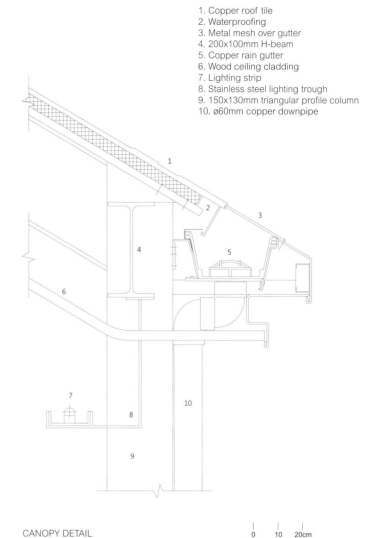

1. Copper roof tile
2. Waterproofing
3. Metal mesh over gutter
4. 200x100mm H-beam
5. Copper rain gutter
6. Wood ceiling cladding
7. Lighting strip
8. Stainless steel lighting trough
9. 150x130mm triangular profile column
10. ø60mm copper downpipe

CANOPY DETAIL

0   10   20cm

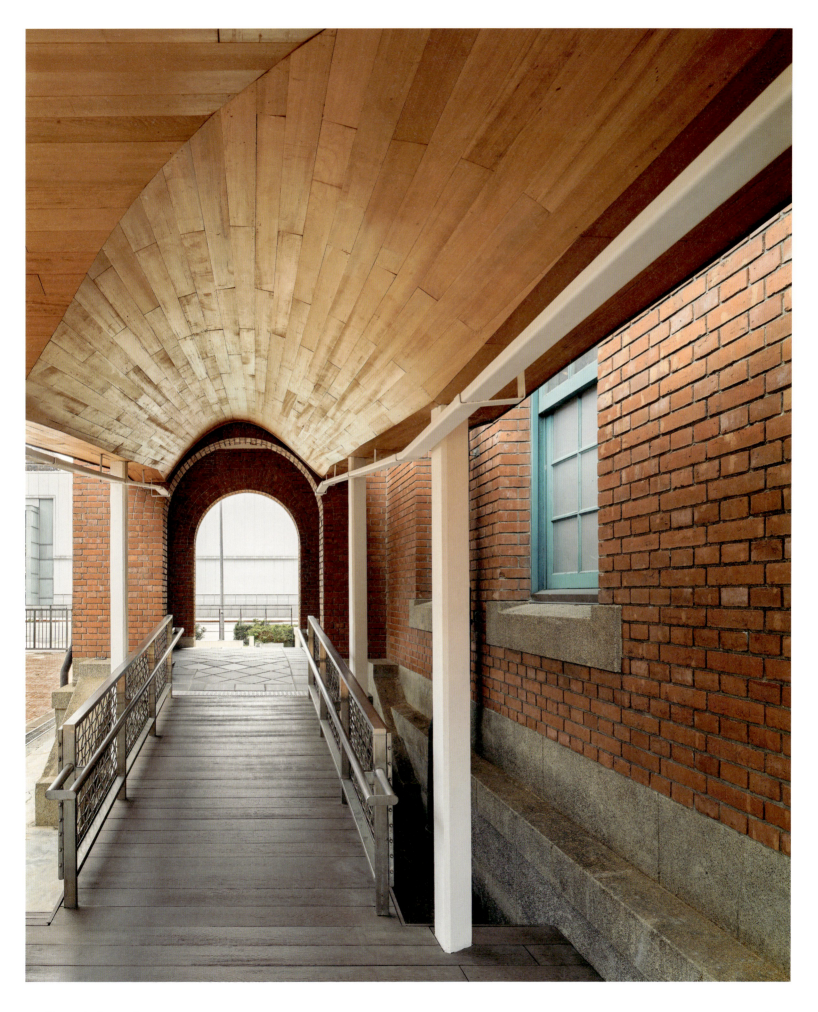

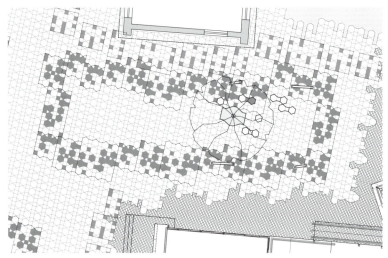

PAVING MODULE PLAN A

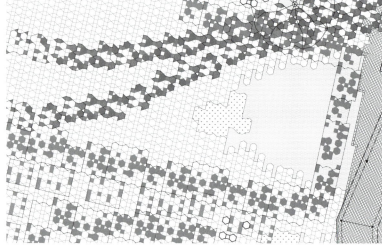

PAVING MODULE PLAN B

The architecture of **xrange**   Inspired by constraints

PAVING MODULE PLAN C

0	1	3	5m	

N

Historical building trace modules

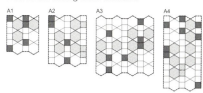

A1 A2 A3 A4

Grey granite
Black granite
White granite
Red granite
Black roof tiles
Yellow granite
Grass area
Ching-Shui red brick

Historical walkway trace modules

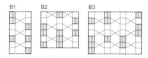

B1 B2 B3

Qing dynasty machine bureau
historical street trace modules

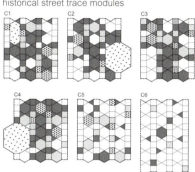

C1 C2 C3

C4 C5 C6

Historical railway trace modules

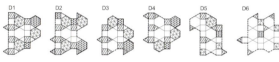

D1 D2 D3 D4 D5 D6

TRACE MODULES

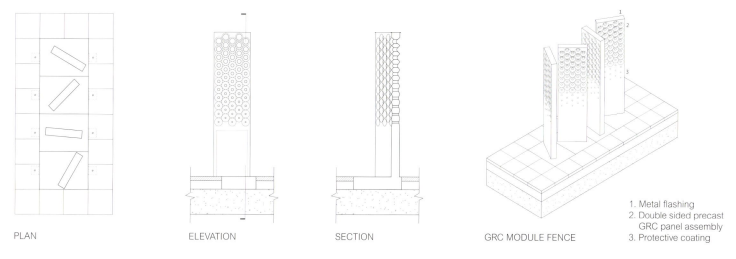

PLAN   ELEVATION   SECTION   GRC MODULE FENCE

1. Metal flashing
2. Double sided precast
   GRC panel assembly
3. Protective coating

— PLAYING tectonics

To borrow from Aaron Betsky's essay, XRANGE's materials palette "tends to emphasize rough, ready-made surfaces and materials brought together for maximum graphic and sensory impact." From **IPEVO Office**, its mesh-sandwiched artificial turf; **XING Mobility Workshop**, an homage to the automobile with transportation related materials; **Gravity Cube/Split Planes** usage of stainless steel mortise and tenon joinery; **C House** with its asymmetric glulam timber stair structure; **Kapok** with recycled wood fiber boards that can be reconfigured as "cards;" **CC Hong Memorial Hall** with its two-sided carved solid oak screens; **Wave Matrix** with interplay of metal waves/light waves; **Amba Hotel** with urban flow/energy that is embedded into its elevations; **Rainbow** with its playful dichroic resin organic elements; and finally **Playpath**, a place of adult/child interaction designed with recycled materials. Materials are often used as experiments or playful tests of spatial effects in various scales, or as tectonic and detailing studies.

IPEVO Office
— See what I see

For the new corporate headquarters of IPEVO, the industry leader in education technology, XRANGE designs a vibrant, high contrast color blocking interior in green, white and black with multiple plays on visual perceptions in homage to the company's document cameras for teaching or demos and their tag line "See what I see." In the space, expanses of turf hover in metal mesh and a logo fragmented into space, alongside elements that reverse weight and depth expectations.

At the lobby, the corporate logo is fragmented and dispersed onto windows, doors and walls of meeting rooms at the far end of the space, its entirety only visible from one specific spot at the reception desk. A blackboard wall provides a changing canvas for the company's products and user stories, its white display shelves are actually the company's name in the form of morse code, another play on perception.

A central green box encloses the staff kitchen and service areas to mark the communal core. The green enclosure is created by sandwiching turf between expanded metal sheets which are used as both structure and "frame" for the turf; a paper thin effect that floats the turf aloft. The floating turf, a large built-in planter box for real trees, clerestory shelves for artificial foliage and glass tables supported by tree trunks surround this central space. Here, the dining tables and a heavy, raw timber bar table rests on "ghosted" metal mesh supports. At the far end of this space, the prototyping area is cordoned off with translucent industrial strip curtain typically used in warehouses.

In the CEO office is the Shelf of Cards, a unique furniture piece designed by XRANGE made of wood fibers impregnated with organic coloring agents. The Shelf of Cards can be reconfigured into various profile combinations that can be horizontal or at an angle. An elongated, vertical painting nook turns out to be a secret space that houses a private changing room and meditation space.

XING Mobility Workshop
— Race forward workshop with local edge

For the work space of renowned EV battery system innovator, XING Mobility, XRANGE's design concept defies convention by defining the auto-tech workshop as a cross between a tech firm, an art gallery, a maker lab and a race car garage, accented with unique details inspired by driving and cars. With just 8 weeks for design and construction on a shoe-string budget for the vast 650 sqm space, gritty, industrial materials are reinterpreted and repurposed as key design elements to sit alongside futuristic electric car parts of carbon fiber and precision engineered titanium, used also by luxury watch makers.

Taking inspiration from the startup's Taiwanese roots, local car and road elements are worked into unique design details throughout the space. Through a very large set of see-through garage doors at the entry, the light filled space is accented with transportation and traffic related colors and motifs.

White traffic reflector sheeting clads enormous sliding garage doors, while a rolling wall partition of orange traffic reflectors sits between the lobby and coffee bar. Blue arrow road signs line the lobby, under which pistons of spent petroleum engines are displayed as reminders of a greasy past. The reception desk is reworked from discarded steel chassis plates; in the bathroom, large clusters of truck rear-view mirrors are repurposed as an array of vanity mirrors. Stair balustrades clad in recycled compressed wood chip boards reveal an existing bollard, painted blue, inside. Custom polyester "fringes" lining the boardroom ceiling is a fire rated, upgraded reinterpretation of the tawdry yet ubiquitous fringe netting used in Taiwanese parking lots and gas stations as sun shading. In the open plan work space, work bays are cordoned off by camouflage netting to obscure sensitive information while simultaneously forming the backdrop to the central "hero car" show area.

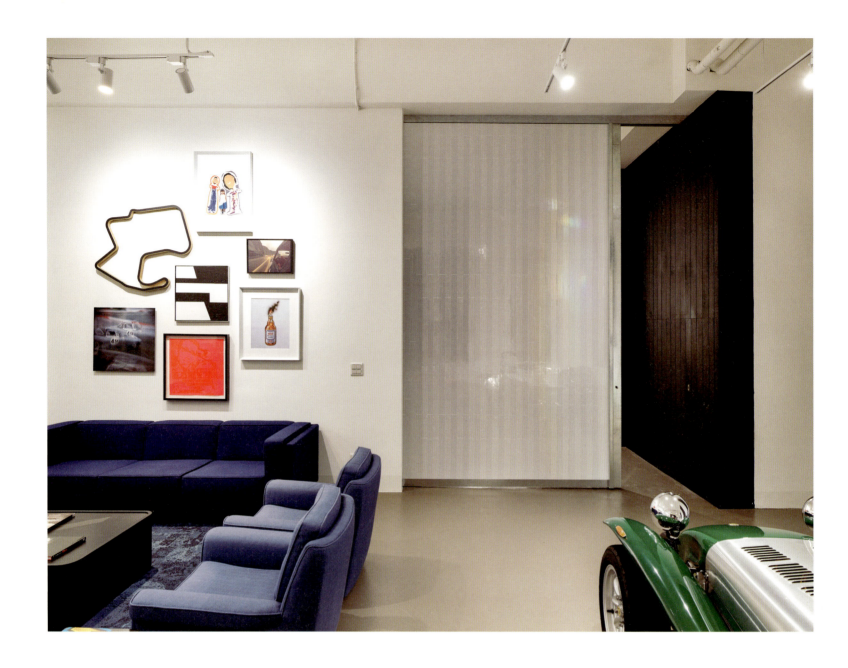

The architecture of **xrange**   Inspired by constraints

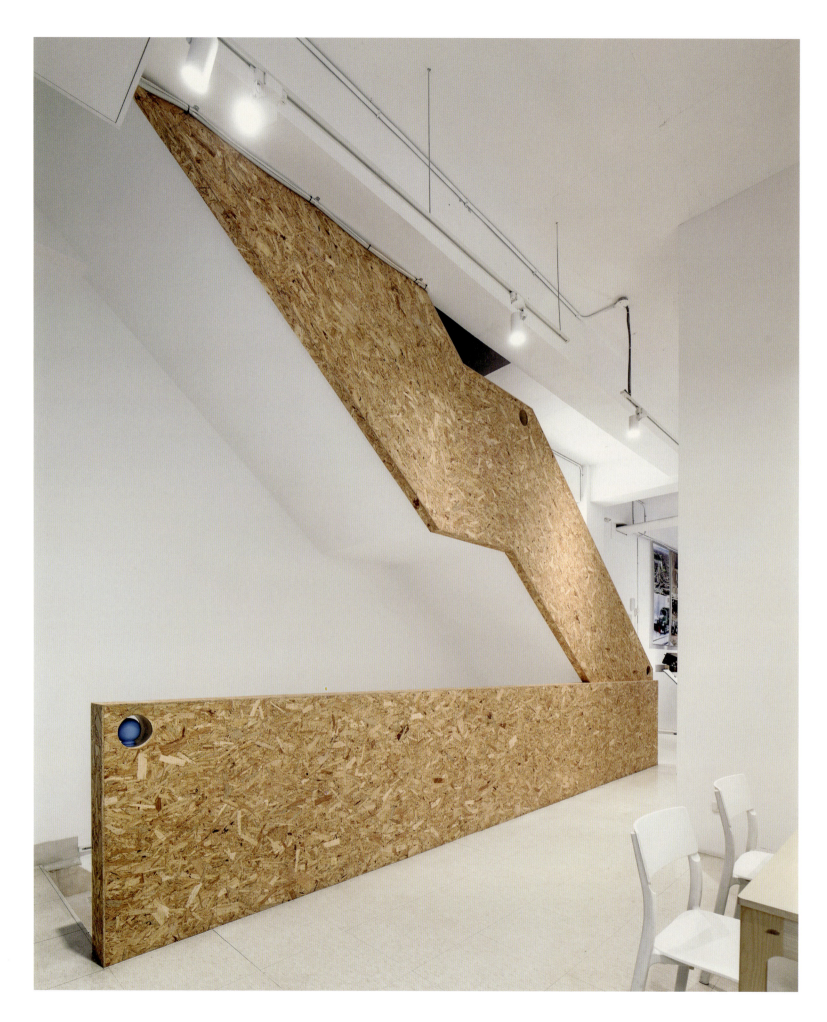

The architecture of **xrange**   Inspired by constraints

Gravity Cube / Fracture Planes
— Stainless steel stage sets, Little Ant & Robot

Designed for the internationally renowned choreographer Huang Yi and his dance studio, Gravity Cube and Fracture Planes is a stage set for the performance "Little Ant & Robot." The performance is a multi sensory experience that melds robotic arms and dancers in a setting inspired by Pina Bausch's Cafe Mueller. Tactile, antique furniture and elements were used throughout the performance, so the architectural sets were designed for elevated, inorganic and stark contrasts, a nod to imageries from Stanley Kubrick's *2001*.

Gravity Cube is a 3x3x3m stainless steel frame composed of 12 parts that is held together by gravity, and can be assembled or dismantled by hand without the use of any tools such as screwdrivers. To fulfill the studio's traveling and stage requirements, Gravity Cube can fit into traveling equipment luggages and 12 person passenger elevators without the need for special loading or tools. Special joinery details were developed based on the mortise and tenon principle. With the weight of the stainless steel itself, Gravity Cube not only can handle equipment loading, but will also support other set pieces in the future. Once assembled, there is no visible trace of connections or joints.

Fracture Planes is a 3x3m mirror titanium coated stainless steel wall composition that challenges presence and perception. In front of it, dancers seem to appear from nowhere, or stand in front of the mirror array without any reflections. Two color tones, black and gold, were used for the titanium coating, and each "plane" or panel is set ajar to the others at a slight angle both horizontally and vertically.

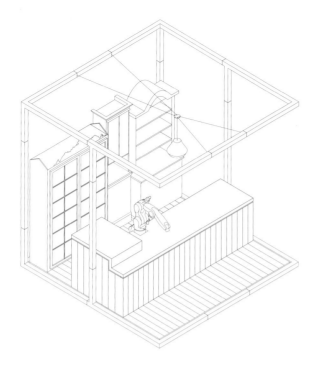

PERFORMANCE INSTALLATION

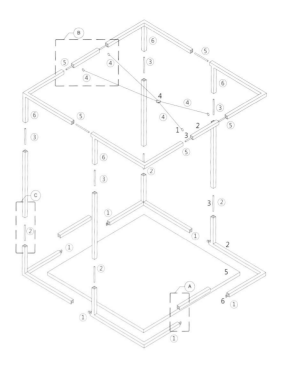

EXPLODED-VIEW OF STRUCTURAL JOINTS

1. Hanging cable
2. Stainless steel tube, □-8x8x0.3t
3. Stainless steel pipe, Ø2.5cm
4. Stainless steel plate with holes for cables
5. Baseplate
6. Stainless steel dovetail joint

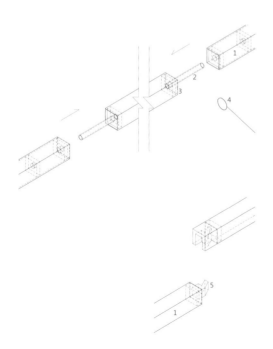

GRAVITY CUBE CONNECTORS

1. Stainless steel tube, □-8x8x0.3t
2. Stainless steel pipe, ø2.5cm
3. Cable hole
4. Hanging cable
5. Stainless steel dovetail joint

GRAVITY CUBE CONNECTORS

1. Stainless steel tube, □-8x8x0.3t
2. Stainless steel pipe, ø2.5cm

The architecture of **xrange**   Inspired by constraints

C House
— Big L little X / two-faced L

Warm wood wraps the interior of the apartment to soften the existing jagged glass front walls. In the double height living space, an asymmetrical spiral staircase constructed from CLT (cross-laminated timber) and steel is a main focus. The stairs are suspended by a curved "L" shaped CLT hanger with embedded steel connectors, and supported at the widest curve by an 8x8cm "x" shape steel rod, a dynamic structural design element that hovers over views of river and skyline. Above the living and open kitchen area is a children's play room shielded by a Hand-cranked L-shaped screen with two faces, solid wood or perforated stainless steel, to vary light conditions.

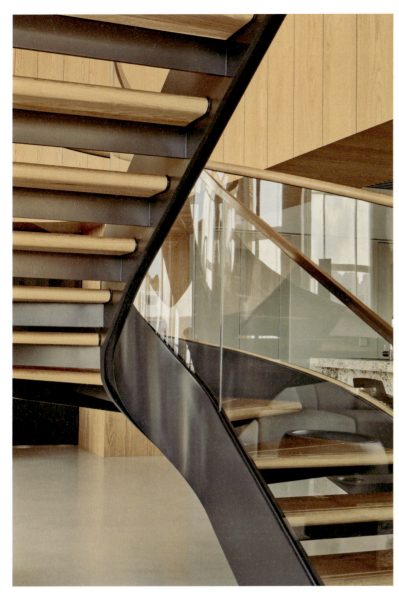

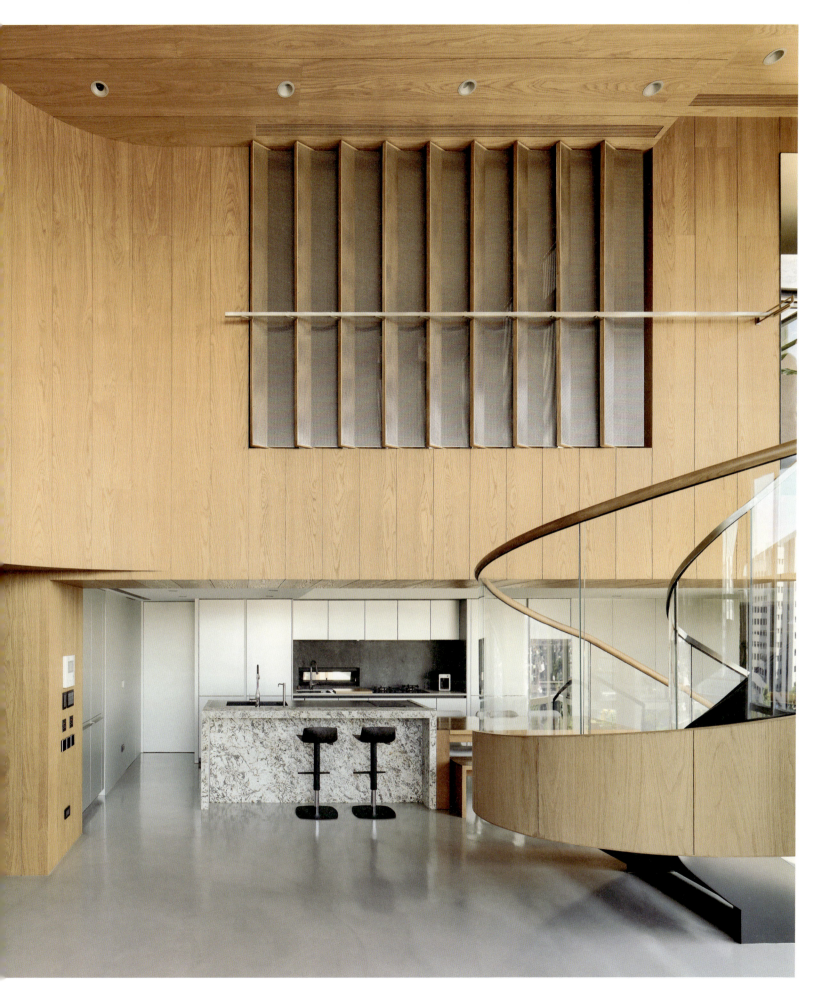

Wave Matrix
— Shed of light wave / metal wave

Inspired by the curves and grills of automobiles, stainless steel strips of 20cm width are grommeted and threaded together to form the roof design of a garage shed. With an unpainted hairline finish, the wave matrix design creates the effect of shimmering patterns of light and shadows throughout the day, echoing the chrome elements and the sinuous lines of the owner's serious car collection. Minimal, geometric and unitized, the wave matrix is fabricated and assembled in a factory and installed on site. The wave matrix is an experiment in utilizing industrial, lo-tech, inexpensive materials and methods with minimal site work to create unique and stunning effects.

The shed is supported by periphery columns clearing a 12.5m x 10m span space within for free form parking. Kept at a low height without obstructing the hacienda style main house built around the late 60s, the shed sits stealthily below the main grounds and overlooks an organic farming patch.

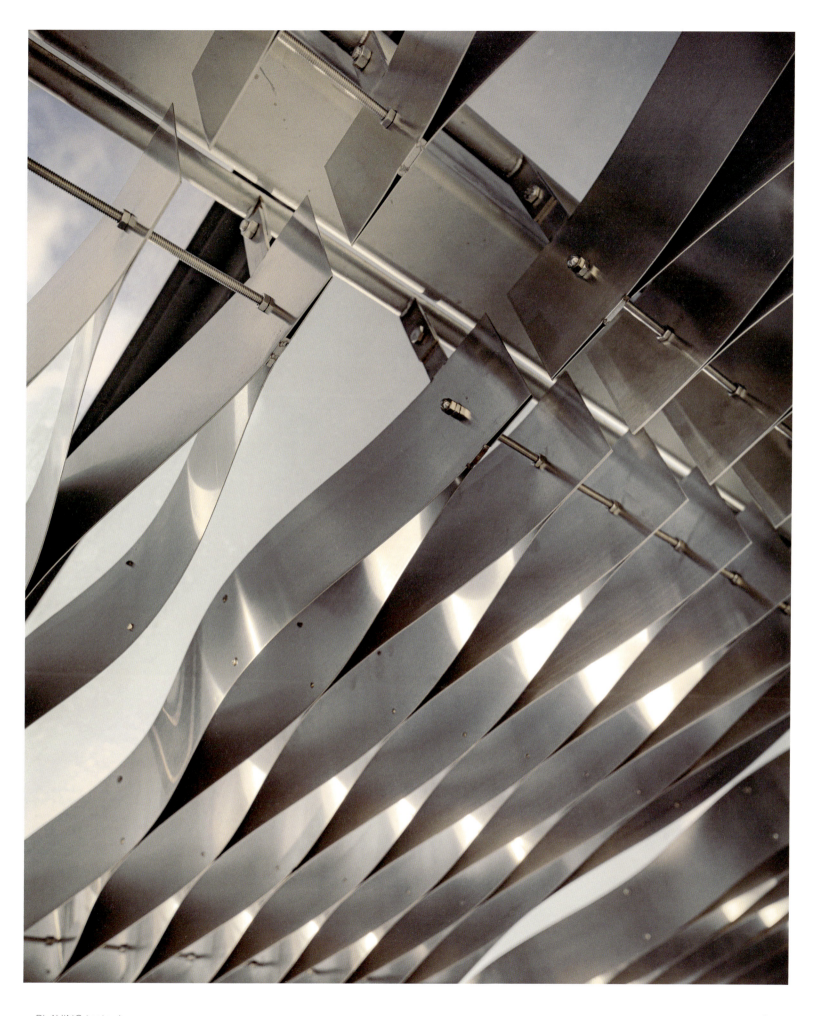

The architecture of **xrange**   Inspired by constraints

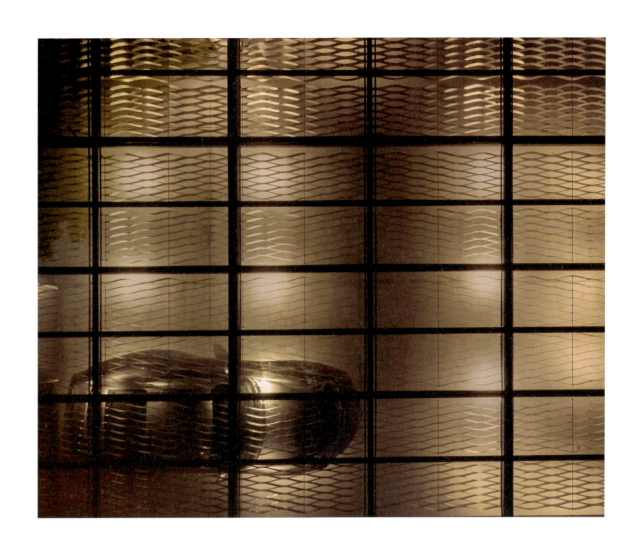

KAPOK
— Shop of Cards

A shop of unique Shelf of Cards systems, a flexible building system made of recycled materials, expresses the Kapok spirit and the ever changing mix of its quality goods sourced from all over the world. The Shelf of Cards is inspired by "house of cards" toys, and is conceived to eliminate on-site construction and material waste. All components are factory cnc-milled and slot-fitted to create freestanding structures of up to 240cm tall. The 200m^2 shop was installed in a mere 5 hours.

The Shelf of Cards system is made from FSC and PEFC certified recycled post-industrial wood fibre panels impregnated with organic dyes. The wall units have slotted column structures and various diversely different shelf profiles such as built-in hangers, cut outs or protruding highlight perches, etc. to accommodate Kapok's multiple product types. The floor units can be dismantled into 10 identical flat panels, and assembled via special criss-crossed slots into different assembly variations.

Standing in space are robust plywood K-frames derived from Kapok's logo. The structure is formed by the emergent branching of multiple Ks made either of square stainless steel tubes, recycled wood fibre panels or birch-ply. The Ks lean against each other for stability and support, forming an interconnected system of weights and counterbalances.

Under the playful kit-of-parts, game-like atmosphere of the Kapok shop are a bespoke, highly interchangeable and expandable shop system. Furthermore, the Shelf of Cards panels even emit the distinctive, pleasant scent of colored pencils, evoking memories of child's play and tactile toys.

PLAN

0 0.5 1   2m

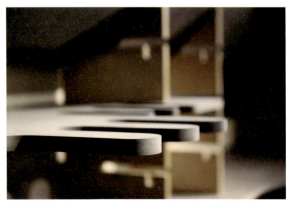

The architecture of **xrange**   Inspired by constraints

AMBA Hotel
— Flow as urban effect

Amba is a 200 room boutique hotel inspired by its exciting site Shimenting—a place of vibrant youth energy, dizzying signages and high foot traffic. The hotel's design concept interprets the seething chaos of the dynamic site into a 10-story urban effect of flow patterns visible from blocks away.

Refurbished from a derelict, 30 year old shopping mall, the massive urban block was overhauled and replanned as a budget hotel for young travelers and backpackers. Room numbers and layouts were constantly adjusted by the clients to align with their business plan over a very tight construction schedule, so the elevation design must react immediately to any, and frequent changes underway. Scripting is used to derive the flow pattern on the building quickly and "naturally." A highly effective means to change in tandem with the client's business unit regarding window numbers and sizes, the design method also systematized and rationalized the existing ad hoc openings and vents. Scripting used here absorbs façade irregularities as movement criteria, then maps them into quantitative parameters, to finally transcribe them into construction drawings for the façade.

Sandwiched between tall buildings, the Street Salon is the outdoor urban lobby and bar entrance to the hotel. It is wrapped in a skin of custom polyester fringes that flow and sway to the wind. The "fringes" are a fire rated, upgraded reinterpretation of the tawdry yet ubiquitous fringe netting used in Taiwanese parking lots and gas stations as sun shading. After dark, the fringes are transformed into a soft haze lit by fiber optics that flicker like twinkling stars.

The architecture of **xrange**   Inspired by constraints

Integration of triangular size (vertical division) and windows size

Southern facade

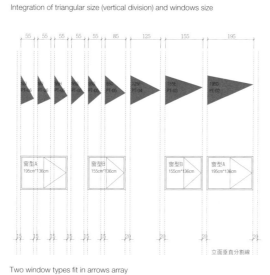

Two window types fit in arrows array

ARROWS WINDOWS INTEGRATION

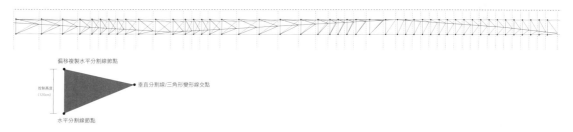

偏移複製水平分割線節點

控制高度
(120cm)

垂直分割線/三角形變形線交點

水平分割線節點

ARROW SETTING

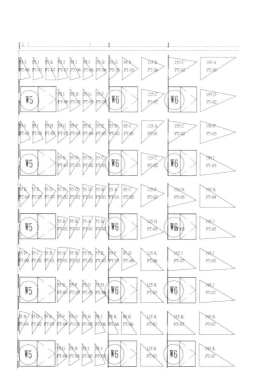

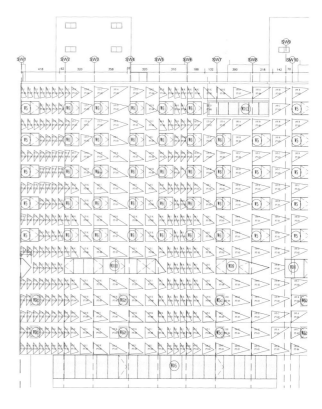

CONSTRUCTION DRAWING

CC Hong Memorial Hall
— The embedded memorial

The project is a memorial hall dedicated to Mr. CC Hong, founder of National, one of Asia's most renowned home electronics brands which later became Panasonic Taiwan. The memorial hall is the penthouse centerpiece to the National Taiwan University College of Management, with a 200-seat conference facility, faculty lounge and offices. Launched in tandem with a lecture program, CC Hong Memorial Hall is conceived as a dynamic learning space rather than a static monument, to be used daily by students and faculty.

Inspired by radio waves (Mr. CC Hong started out as a radio repairman), XRANGE creates a commemoration space crafted entirely from solid oak columns, with a mural "story" told by variegated striations of light and shadow.

The memorial hall is "inscribed" with CC Hong's portrait and the two iconic streetscapes that captured his legacy, the Hong Foundation (founded in 1972) and the enormous "National" neon sign that once dominated the heart of old Taipei for a decade from the 70s to the 80s. By way of historical photographs, the iconic images were transcribed and melded into the space as a subtle yet distinct presence as wall, mural and screen all at once. The image murals were made as a three dimensional spatial imprint, as negative cut-outs from 300 pieces of densely placed 4x15x240cm solid oak columns that are carved on both faces. A total of 600 oak columns were used in the entire space.

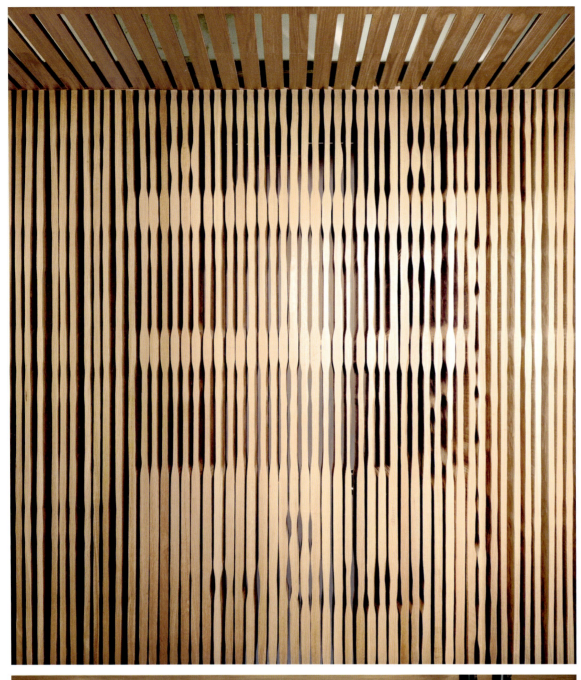

Rainbow
— Hinged petals of recycled dichroic resin

Rainbow is a room partition made of eco resin repurposed from PET with a dichroic screen sandwiched between two 5mm resin layers. Each uniquely shaped panel is fabricated in the manufacturer's USA plant then shipped to Taiwan for installation. Organic, free form floral shapes are hung from cables, and hinge or pivot over each other with custom fabricated stainless steel hardware.

The organic tiling maximizes the color nuances of the material; every subtle change in hinge angle is registered as an unpredictable yet dramatic color change to fully express and capture the properties of the diachronic resin. Depending on the time of day and the amount of indoor lighting, the screen changes from serene white and gold tones to bright orange, cyan, purple and pink.

The architecture of **xrange**   Inspired by constraints

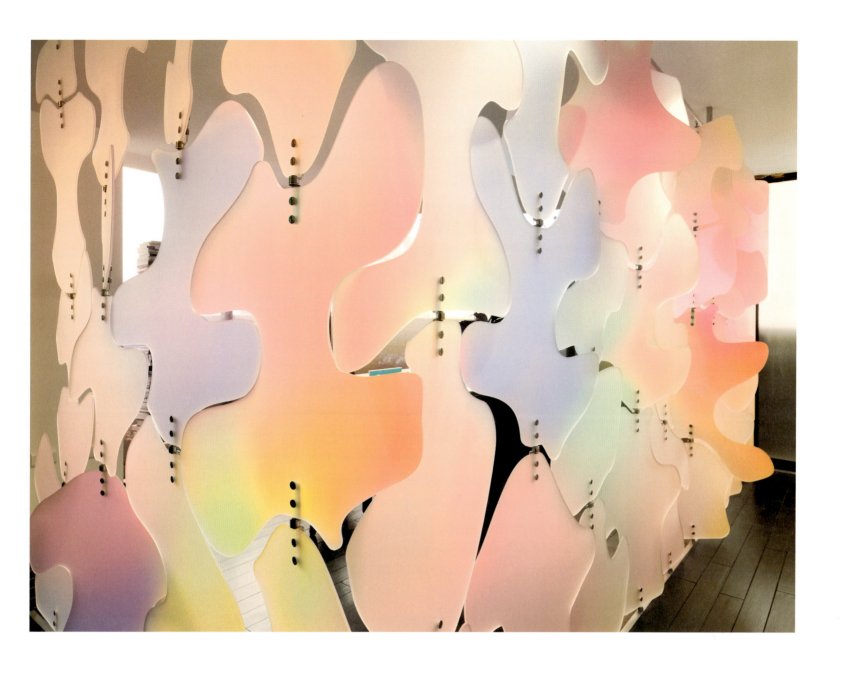

Playpath
— Curious forms for explorations

Located in downtown Taipei, in a park adjacent to the City Hall, Playpath connects to a larger urban network of open spaces between big box retail malls that draw large crowds on weekends. The open spaces in the area are passages or busy public thoroughfares with scant public amenities or places of refuge. In addition to its proximity to City Hall and mega malls, Playpath is also edged by large office buildings and hotels on a site next to a former performance theater now demolished.

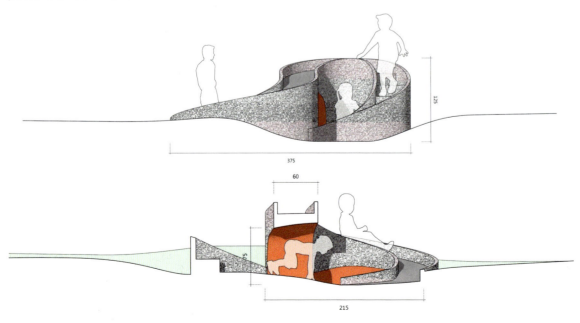

PLAN

0 1   3   5m

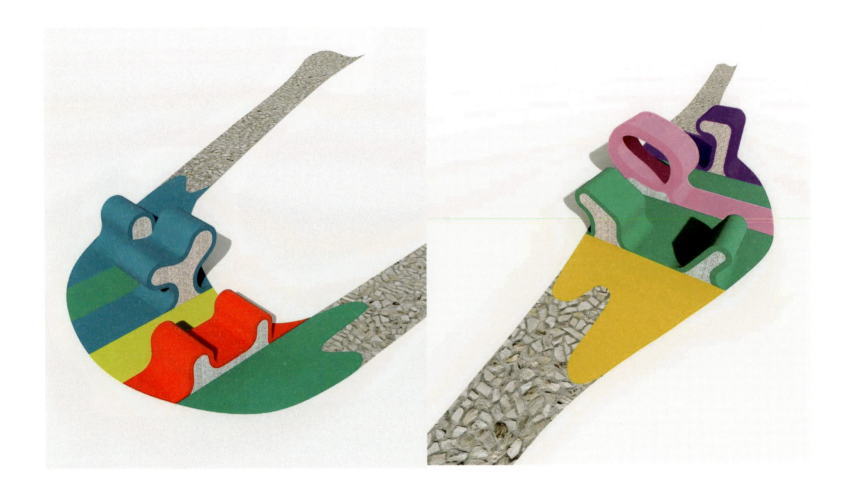

Playpath is therefore conceived as a place of playful interaction between children and adults, a place to stop and wonder, a breather and a place of refuge in the heart of retail and commercial mania. Inspired by the drawings of imaginary places in children books, the design explores curiosity beyond words, creating surreal landscape forms in the otherwise characterless park.

A garden path with nodes of colorful protrusions from the ground, the wavy forms invite

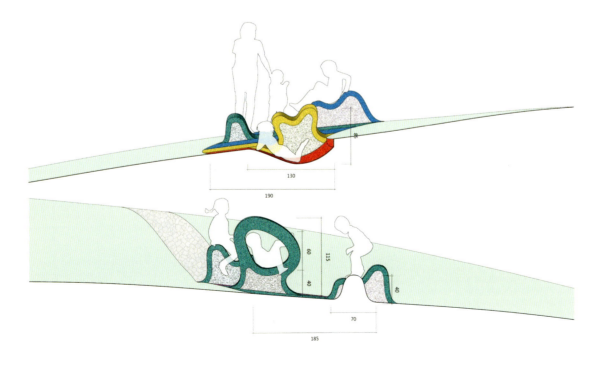

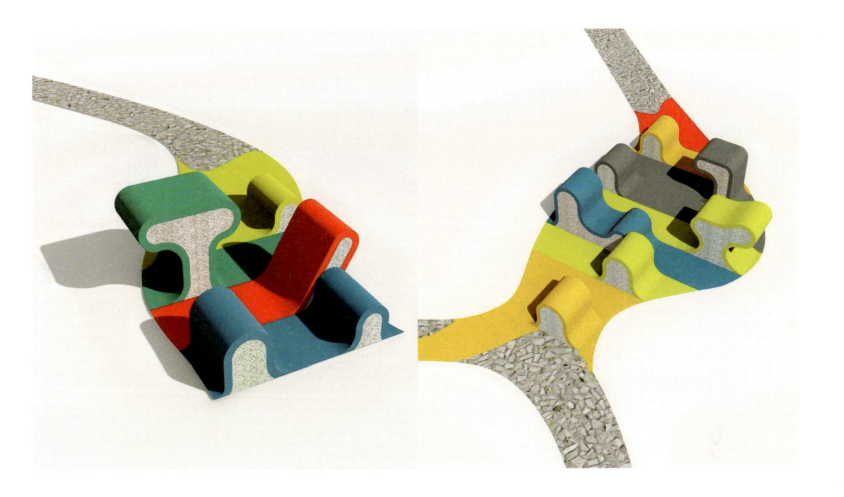

children to explore and investigate. They are made out of recycled PU material used on running tracks, firm but soft to the touch. The elements' dimensions are scaled for use by multiple generations, encouraging them to react with their bodies in any way comfortable, uncomfortable, weird or challenging. As such this playful ensemble invites interactive "performances" from both children and adults while offering a place of relaxation and respite in the heart of a teeming city.

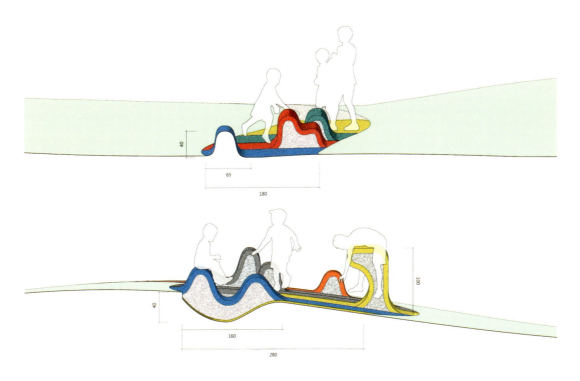

Interview — James Moore McCown & Grace Cheung

James Moore McCown: Grace, thanks so much for taking the time to speak with me.

Grace Cheung: You're most welcome.

JMc: Talk to me about growing up in Malaysia and then going to Canada. Was it that that inspired you to become an architect? What were your parents' professions?

GC: I grew up in a really small town in Malaysia. My parents are first- and second-generation Chinese immigrants. My father was originally from China, and he had traveled during the Cultural Revolution to Hong Kong and Thailand. My dad was a musician. And my mother was one of the first women to work at the Hong Kong and Shanghai Bank in our hometown.

In our small town, it was a simple life. We didn't really have much. I had two sisters and a brother. We were always finding things to do and inventing our own games and stuff like that. What inspired me to be an architect? I didn't even know the word "architecture" until I was 17. I'd never even heard of it. I wanted to be an artist.

I had always loved to draw and was always making stuff. But in my hometown, there was no role model. I was like, oh, maybe I should be a fashion designer. At school, my grades were considered pretty good. I knew how to take exams the Asian way.

So the teachers thought that I could have a career as a doctor. And so my parents, of course, being very traditional, said yes, be a doctor. And I didn't object to it because I love science, I love physics, I love biology. Eventually we went to Canada, actually first stop being Winnipeg to attend grade 13.

That summer, I went to the library with my sister because there was nothing to do, and then I saw a book. It was a tiny book on the modern masters Le Corbusier, Walter Gropius, Frank Lloyd Wright and Mies van der Rohe. And that was the first time I saw the word "architecture." The book had no color, and very few pictures of projects. It was a small book. And I remember at that point, at 17; I realized that this is my calling in life.

JMc: You've lived on three continents, Europe, Asia and America. So give me a sense of how you see yourself. Are you Chinese or are you a global citizen?

GC: I think I am definitely a global citizen. I think I could live

pretty much in most places. But growing up as an immigrant Chinese or what we call Overseas Chinese, there is definitely a large part of the culture ingrained in me. In most places where there is kind of a strong Asian presence, like Vancouver, or I think anywhere in Europe or America, it would be quite easy for me to settle in. There is a Western way of communicating and there's also a more Asian way.

JMc: Isn't that interesting? Now, I know you went to Columbia for grad school. Where did you do your undergraduate work?

GC: University of Manitoba, which is in Winnipeg. It's in the middle of Canada and cold, extremely cold. I went from very warm tropical temperatures to -25 degrees.

JMc: Absolutely. So tell me how you ended up in Taiwan. Did you have relatives there? Or was it that you thought there were a lot of opportunities on the island?

GC: Actually, it's kind of interesting because I think throughout my entire life, architecture has always been kind of my North Star. It actually took some effort to get into architecture school because I had wanted to transfer as soon as I knew I wanted to be an architect. So from science/pre-med to architecture. From that point onward, I think I had always followed where architecture takes me. For me, it was everything I had ever wanted to do. After graduation, I worked in New York and then Hong Kong. It's all because of work. And then that got me to Hong Kong to work for OMA Asia and then to Rotterdam with Office for Metropolitan Architecture (OMA). And there was a project that I was assigned to at OMA in Hong Kong. It was a service station, a highway rest stop in Taiwan.

So I was assigned the project, went to Taiwan and met some people there, who turned out to be my future husband's high school friends, and so because of that, I met my husband and I ended up staying. So it was through architecture, I think, that I kind of found my "family."

JMc: In your TED Talk, you mentioned a building in Taipei that's all stairs. And you were enamored of that. Talk to me about why.

GC: Why do I love that building so much? I think there is something very impossible about it. To design a building that is just full of stairs on one face. I think with the kind of rational training that we've gone through, something like this probably wouldn't happen. There's something very irrational, but very emotional, very unusual and amazing about this structure. I still think it's one of the most incredible buildings ever.

JMc: You mentioned in the TED Talk that you're always being asked by people, "Why is Taipei so ugly?" Do you think it's ugly or is it just capitalism taken to its extreme with advertising everywhere? Advertising on the buildings, advertising in the streets. Talk to me about Taipei and how you feel about it.

GC: I think on a certain level, it's ugly. It has a lot of similarities to places like Hong Kong where you have a lot of advertising. Taipei is different in that it has a lot more alleyways that you can venture into. In the alleyways, things become very green, more comfortable, more naturalistic. I think Taipei is probably one of the greenest cities I've lived in. There are parks and trees everywhere. But it does retain a lot of the out-of-control crazy "Asianess" to it.

I'm always interested in seeing in that kind of urban context how people improvise or how they use the space. That's also why I made up the term "urbanmatic" for urban automatic, like urban magic. I think no architect would be able to create these sorts of phenomena. But they somehow share a certain common attitude or common language. So it's very exciting to observe moments like that. And then sometimes those ideas directly or indirectly would inspire me to do certain things. Maybe I see it because I'm still a foreigner in a way. Although I've lived in Taiwan for 20 years, I am still a global citizen.

JMc: You touched upon the "urbanmatic" trope. I'd love to hear more about that. What do you mean by it?

GC: Everywhere you go, you see how certain spaces form on their own. To give you an example, everyone knows the Wan Chai district in Hong Kong. It's kind of like a bar area where a lot of people go and hang out. In the evening people just spilled onto the streets to drink. There you would see this sort of intervention by everyday people where they would take the traffic barrier on the sidewalk to create a makeshift bar so people could lean on it. And so those are the things that I find very exciting because they're very dynamic. They're always changeable, always depending on people.

JMc: It's architecture without architects, in a way.

GC: Exactly, these are like urban phenomena that just happen on their own. It's not designed by anybody, and I find that exciting.

JMc: Also, in the TED Talk, that was this amazing residential house project that you talked about. And I found it beautiful, very sculptural. Can you explain how the morphology of it came about? Talk to me about that house and who was the client? What was the program?

GC: The house is on the east coast of Taiwan island facing the Pacific Ocean, and in a region prone to typhoons. That area is incredibly beautiful, the climate is very nice and people just generally spend a lot of time outdoors.

JMc: Most of the time it's a tropical climate.

GC: A tropical climate, yes. But when the typhoon comes, it usually makes landfall there. So this sort of tropical fantasy, you know, if you think it's like Bali, it's actually not quite that. So things have to be very securely locked down when typhoons come, and it does happen every summer. The idea of protection becomes a kind of main driving force for the concept, as the client wanted a weekend house, and he wanted to have this sort of outdoor living.

The house is kind of designed like a cage, which is a rigid shell that could be locked down so that when typhoon comes, all the living arrangements which are mostly outdoors, can be protected; the cage also protects the inner shell which is the sun shading and insect netting because the client is very insect phobic. And so that's how the idea came about. But what I was really excited about was that the house really now no longer becomes like a house per se, but it's like this sort of protective caging where inside the living programs are separated into their own little prefab boxes.

The form of the house echoes the mountains behind.

JMc: How far is it from Taipei?

GC: You have to take the plane for an hour and then about another 40 minutes by car. And it's an area where lots of artists and cultural people live. Yeah, it's sort of an artsy, bohemian enclave. A lot of people from Taipei like to live there because it's very beautiful.

JMc: What do you call the project?

GC: It's called Beetle House.

JMc: Super. Let's talk about the Penghu house. What about that house and what inspired it?

GC: Generations of the client's family are from Penghu Island, a small island.

JMc: Right off of Taiwan. Is that right?

GC: Yes. The client founded his own business on the main island of Taiwan and had success. He wanted to "return home" and build a house for his family and for him to go stay on weekends. And so I wanted to give the house a sort of ancestral home significance.

This is like the proud son returning home; he wanted the house to speak of permanence, that he had made it and he'd come a long way. On Penghu Island they have these houses from the Qing Dynasty. They're historical structures, nobody lives in them now. These houses are made of stacked coral stone, and they have this Qing dynasty coastal architecture rolled roof gables, which is basically a pitched roof, but with these curved or rolled roof ridges.

But I didn't want to copy the kind of old coral houses because this then wouldn't make sense for him or for me. So I referenced the impression of a cluster of these houses. There's a historical park on the island where these houses are clustered. There you see them above the grass line with this distinctive roof profile, and that became the inspiration of the house. I took the nine square plan, but instead of making an open courtyard in the middle, I made it into sort of a grand central hall that you see. This is the gathering space for the family on Chinese New Year and on other festival days, when they would put up round tables and have a feast.

JMc: Wow. Absolutely. You must really like the Wandering Walls project because I believe it's on the cover of the monograph. Am I correct? You must talk to me about that project. You must like it. And what is the program? What is the project for? Who are the clients?

GC: The project is a small bed and breakfast. It has seven rooms, the client also lives there. The client is actually a travel blogger. He's traveled around the world and it took him about two years to find the site on the mountain. Generally, when we talk about the south of Taiwan, usually it's about the sea and people doing all kinds of ocean activities.

This site is on the other side of the peninsula, overlooking the ocean on a mountaintop. The client wanted to have a place that, according to him, that you cannot find in the city. On top of that, when we first visited the site, there was no road, there was nothing around. There are severe winter winds. The client has very, very little budget to do this. When I went to the site, I really fell in love with the rawness of it, the grassland on the mountain top and the indigenous acacia trees. I wanted to use the most minimal means, for example, one singular architectural element, which are the walls. The walls are a kind of wind barrier, the walls are also the interior and exterior because we didn't have budget for interior finishes.

JMc: But it's this rough board formed concrete. Yes, that's very gritty. Very rough. What does that mean to you as an architect?

GC: I think it was quite a challenge to kind of let go and do that because, yes, those are really the cheapest formwork you can find.

Anyway, yes, they are low grade formworks, but in a way because at that location down south, there was no way we could have gotten good quality workmanship or a professional construction team. Those were out of the question. We can only use what we call "cement workers," people who are just in the trade, who would come in and do the work. So I knew that not being able to control the quality would be a key aspect from very early on.

So we needed to make this rawness part of the design language and not control it like we would normally, such as, having the formwork to be in a certain way, or to be a certain smoothness.

JMc: And it's formed with wood boards. Am I correct?

GC: Exactly. And also, there wasn't any way for them to be able to make actual curved walls. So we made them out of flat boards. But then in a kind of system where we would go from 30 cm boards to 4 cm batons depending on the curvature. So I set that as a system and then to let the workers have a way to work it out. Plus they're very prone to not reading drawings. So a lot of it has to be communicated on site. Basically when all the formwork comes off, that would be the building. And that's immensely challenging to do. The building sits on top of the mountain with very strong winds, so now, two years after the project was completed, the exterior, if you touch it with your hand, it's actually very, very smooth.

Smoothed by the wind. But on the inside, when you're inside the room, you can still see the roughness. And I find that so, so fascinating that the building, being there, it feels like it has been there forever. There is a sense of weight and permanence to it.

JMc: No, I see that now. The Japanese influence, the beautiful wood, the undulating ceiling.

GC: With Wandering Walls, I did not start with wanting to make concrete monumental. That wasn't the intention. This was like, it was the only material we could have used for that site. Steel was out of the question.

I was quite pleased that, as rough as the building is, some of these ideas we were able to execute and kind of made this very unusual statement.

JMc: Absolutely. Talk to me about the Winbond building with the glass façade that undulates. Was that for a corporate client? Is it an electric company? And what were you trying to achieve with that design?

GC: They are a huge memory solution provider, one of the bigger chip makers in Taiwan.

The company has been around, I think, for over 30 years, they manufacture chips. So this building is actually meant for their engineers, the high tech workers. They are a very practical minded company. And from the beginning, I knew that I cannot escape cubicles. This had to be done with cubicles to accommodate for more than 2,000 people in that building.

They published a book for their 30th Anniversary, in which they actually spent a few chapters talking about what they call the Winbond Person. They've invested a lot in the wellbeing of their people in terms of health, eco education, and so on. And so I knew this would be a very important topic for the

client, and it's of interest to them to do this. When I visited their old office, they would have these cubicles, but then all the walkways were lined with rows of potted plants, almost like soldiers marching down the aisles.

There is a desire to somehow provide a better, more comfortable, better space for their team so that there's a better sense of collaboration and enhanced creativity. I wanted to pull out some informal spaces to the front of the building. These became social spaces. They're informal spaces, resting spaces. They're also places where people can just hang out and chill out.

JMc: There's a lot of that kind of office design here in the U.S. now. But the curtain wall. Talk about the curtain wall.

GC: That form is actually driven by the desire to create these informal spaces outside of the cubicle, to have some relief from the cubicles.

We put the building through green analysis and realized that all these folds were actually very important shadow pockets. The building performed very, very well in the temperature analysis. It's an eco-green building strategy that was driven by the desire to create more human spaces.

JMc: Absolutely. I'm going to shift gears a little bit and talk about Royce Hong. And how did you meet him? How did you come to form a firm with him?

GC: He's my husband.

JMc: Well, that's wonderful. Congratulations. We have so many husband-and-wife teams here in Boston.

GC: It's interesting because Royce is actually not an architect. He studied industrial design at the Art Center, and graphic design at RISD.

JMc: I love RISD.

GC: In the beginning, we actually had never thought of working together, when we were planning for our wedding, we did a competition together. This was for a trophy design for the Run Run Shaw Foundation in Hong Kong.

JMc: So this is back in 2003?

GC: Yes. So we did a design and we actually won. To our surprise, that was the first time I'd actually designed something that was not architecture. We thought, OK, maybe we should set up an office to see what we can do, and that's what we did. In the beginning, we also did product design and some of them sold really well and so they spun off and became their own company. Royce's language is more entrepreneurial and product driven. I also have a strong interest in art. So it makes us a very atypical architecture office. I've never considered myself a typical architect to begin with.

JMc: Tell me where the name XRANGE came from. And one of your mottos is "Inspired by Constraints." I want to hear about that.

GC: Well, when we formed the office, we called it XRANGE because I tend to do the very big stuff, like architecture, whereas Royce tends to do the very small stuff, like the product design. It's a sort of zooming in, or zooming out, across all sorts of scales.

JMc: I like the name. It's very evocative.

So, again, I want to shift gears a little bit and talk about your love of art. Did you ever consider becoming a painter or a sculptor yourself?

GC: I did, when I was six, I wanted to be an artist. I think by the age of 14, I was able to paint photorealism.

JMc: Wow. Amazing.

GC: I suppose in the end, I ended up being an architect, my true calling in life. To put it very simply, it's because with architecture, I can combine my artistic side and my scientific side. But all these years I have always been excited and inspired by art, especially contemporary art. I mean, I think I always find a lot of interesting stories or nuances or points of view. It's always been kind of a massive hobby.

JMc: And you have a foundation in Taipei. Talk to me about that, how you're very involved in the art scene there.

GC: Yes. The Hong foundation is 50 years old now. It was set up by Royce's grandfather years ago.

So instead of just doing charity relief or helping people, the foundation has a focus on education and the arts. So over the years, we've done quite a lot of sponsorships to rising artists.

JMc: So I see. Giving them grants and so forth?

GC: Yes. Royce's mother ran the foundation for 50 years until last year, when she retired. So now it's come to us to be in charge, I am now the vice chairman and also the executive director of the foundation.

I started sponsoring artists about 8 years ago. I launched several programs to sponsor a wide range of artists, from the very young ones to the very established, kind of like trying to cover more like an ecosystem of creators.

And after eight years in, in time for the Foundation's 50th anniversary this year, we actually worked with the Museum of Contemporary Art in Taipei to put up a show of all these artists that we'd sponsored, with the pieces that we commissioned. It was a big show.

JMc: Amazing.

GC: I've been involved not so much from a design point of view, but from a more curatorial perspective.

JMc: Administrative and curatorial.

GC: Yes.

JMc: Let's talk about your early work experience. You worked for very top firms like Patkau in Canada and Tschumi in New York and of course OMA. What did you learn from those experiences? Was it a very grueling sort of a baptism by fire into architecture or was it very gratifying? Did you learn a lot?

GC: I think I was very lucky.

JMc: Well, these are top firms.

GC: I think my portfolio was good. I don't know, maybe timing. I was a little lucky. Obviously, these are not easy firms to get into.

JMc: Exactly. I think. But you had gone to Columbia. You had a good portfolio?

GC: I suppose. At Patkau, they invested heavily on working out all the design details thoroughly and incessantly, and that was very remarkable to see. At Bernard Tschumi's, it was like nobody actually tells you what to do. You showed up at the office and they were like, oh, this is what we're working with. And so I kind of had to figure out what I could do and what I could bring to the team. I worked on a competition in France which we won.

I didn't stay for the construction phase because by then I had already been in New York for four and some years. I thought it would be time to see something else. So then comes the OMA Asia experience. I was scouted by the person in charge of the office then. I speak Cantonese. So it's like, OK, maybe it's time to go to Asia. I hadn't thought that I would be back in Asia at all at that time. But then I thought it would be kind of a big unknown, to try new things. So I went. And that started my OMA Asia experience.

That was grueling. That was intense. Rem (Koolhaas) encourages this sort of competition, the whole team dukes it out.

JMc: Would he come to the Asia office often?

GC: Not often at that time. He would come like maybe once every few months, and we also flew to Rotterdam to work with the team over there. And of course, the schedule, the schedule was crazy. He would come in at 2 a.m. and we all had to wait for him. And then we talk about the design schemes which were always being scrapped and then we would start from scratch. Everyone was in their twenties, late twenties, early thirties, so there was a lot of power to burn. But it's also a situation where I think it's okay for 5 to 6 years. But beyond that, I think it's really time to start out on your own, which a lot of us did.

I think I have met a lot of good friends there who basically after five or six years, they all started their own offices.

JMc: That's great.

GC: It was great, an exciting environment. You meet all these people from different places, all different cultures. Of course, when I was there, I was like the exotic one, you know, the one from Asia. And I made a lot of good friends.

JMc: So how does your firm get work? Do you just wait for the phone to ring, or do you enter competitions?.

GC: It's really word of mouth. I think we are, at the core, kind of

a service profession. Yes. So I always think, I always believe that, you know, we are in the business of trust, helping clients achieve some very hard things. And so throughout the process, I think you do build trust with the client, and the client's team. And so people tend to come back to us because of word of mouth.

JMc: You're lucky in that regard. How many people do you have in your office?

GC: I have about ten now. I've been keeping my team at about 10 people or so, and at any given point we'd be working on four projects.

JMc: Nice size.

GC: Like between 5 to 10 is ideal.

JMc: Yes. Have you ever worked in the People's Republic of China and what was that experience like?

GC: When I was at OMA Asia and when I was doing some consulting work before founding XRANGE. Way back then, it was quite outlandish, because you would have a design and then two weeks later the client would come back and say, "Oh, the site has changed" and then this whole thing gets plopped onto another site somewhere else, and it's just done so frequently and so nonchalantly.

It was really not about creating meaning or whatever. It's just an economic tool, you know, you're just churning through design. So I found it very draining and very hard to actually explore something deeper. And once the basic design is done, you pass it on to the design institutes and any shape you could draw up, they could build. So it's a very different animal from what we understand architecture to be. Yes, it requires a completely different mindset. I think it's interesting to have seen that. But I know definitely it's not how I would like to devote my energy.

JMc: Yes. So talk to me about this. I know you hate being asked this question. But I have to ask it. Who are your heroes in architecture? Who really inspires you?

GC: Who really inspires me? You know, I went to France to see Le Corbusier's architecture when I was 22.

JMc: Amazing.

GC: It changed my life. I saw La Tourette and the next day the entire land was frosted over. I could not forget the power and the beauty of what I saw.

JMc: Well, La Tourette has this board formed concrete that's very similar to your style.

GC: Well, I wouldn't say it's my style, but this is another point.

And after La Tourette, I saw Ronchamp and I think it blew my mind. And then, of course, I love guys like Oscar Niemeyer.

JMc: I did my graduate thesis on Oscar Niemeyer.

GC: I love him. And also Paulo Mendes de Rocha, I love. I love work like that. Like, for example, Felix Candela.

Because you know what? I love them so much because they work outside of that sort of Western context where you have the technology, you have the talent, you have the means, you have the money to build whatever you want. But outside of, say, America or sort of big European countries, there is no technology, there is no well-trained talent. But they're able to create these timeless, emotional works.

JMc: Well, I think Candela is not publicized enough. I think he's one of the great architects of the 20th century. And you don't hear about him.

GC: And those, most incredible, amazing curved forms that he built.

JMc: Yes.

GC: I look at these guys from Paraguay. You know, some of the work that is coming out of there, I think it really captures this aspect of architecture that is so powerful, so emotional, so tactile. You can call it regionalism, but I think it's much more than that. It's really taking very little means, but creating these amazing, amazing moving spaces for the people and the different cultures. And I think that gives me tremendous inspiration.

JMc: Well, you mentioned Niemeyer and Candela in Latin America, the labor is cheap, so it's perfect for concrete. The structure of the buildings is very daring.

GC: So I think definitely my Wandering Walls project was really driven by that sort of desire. When you build outside of Taiwan island or in the outlying areas outside of big cities, you do face a lot of these local factors. Cultural contingencies, like you really cannot predict what's going to happen, how they're going to take it, how they're going to react and what they're willing to do. You have to be highly flexible. You know, like any time there is a change, you have to quickly adapt, but still hold on to the central spirit of the architecture that you want to build.

JMc: Yes. Talk to me about New York. Did you not like it there? You referred to it as a concrete jungle. I was living there at the same time because I was there in the nineties, when there was little crime and a strong economy.

GC: Did I like it? It is a place that was not very easy for me. I mean, I definitely saw the lowbrow side of New York. I was a poor student. It's not like I had money.

It was definitely gritty. There was a lot of raw energy. There were all types of cultures coming together. Things were not always friendly. I was followed on the street like three times, you know, being a single woman.

JMc: How many languages do you speak?

GC: I speak English, Mandarin and Cantonese, some Malay and Hakka, another southern Chinese dialect. I would call Cantonese my native language.

JMc: The language in Malaysia. Is it Cantonese?

GC: Yes. I spoke Cantonese as a child with my family.

My mother tongue is Cantonese. It turns out the hometown that I grew up in was nicknamed Little Hong Kong. There were a lot of Cantonese immigrants there, so I spoke Cantonese as a child. Then I moved to North America. So obviously English very quickly became a second language. By now, it's half my first language, the other half being Cantonese. And when I came to Taiwan, my Mandarin was so rusty I could barely put together a sentence. But now I speak Mandarin, I can lecture in Mandarin, write in Mandarin. So I speak these three consistently and daily.

JMc: How does it work? If you were born in Malaysia, do you have to apply for citizenship in Taiwan or are you still a Malaysian?

GC: For a few years after we immigrated, in order to keep the Malaysian passport, we would have to go back to Malaysia to renew it at the time. So our family decided to just give up on the Malaysian citizenship. Now I travel as a Canadian citizen, and a foreigner resident in Taiwan.

JMc: Wow. Well, great. Well, Grace, thank you so much for taking the time to talk to me.

GC: You're quite welcome. My pleasure.

James Moore McCown is a Boston-based architectural journalist who writes for numerous design publications including *Metropolis*, *Architect's Newspaper* and *AD PRO Architectural Digest*. He has collaborated with Oscar Riera Ojeda on several books including the Architecture in Detail series which comprised four volumes: *Elements, Materials, Colors* and *Spaces*. McCown studied journalism at Loyola University New Orleans and holds an ALM (Master's Degree) in the history of art and architecture from Harvard University, where his thesis on modern Brazilian architecture received an Honorable Mention, Dean's Award, Best ALM Thesis (2007). He lives in Newton, Massachusetts.

Afterword — Grace Cheung

Architecture begins with an idea, an idea about experience, movement and space. This idea also embodies the architecture's ambition, intent and purpose. The compounding of all the above creates the conceptual formwork or organizing principles of architecture that excites me the most. I call this conceptual framework "story form," which brackets the essence of the building endeavor in creating architecture. From "story form," the entire framework of complex building systems can germinate, aspects such as structure, light and shadow, materials, circulation patterns, mechanical services etc. At this very beginning of the idea, form can be the simplest, purest, clearest expression of desire, enclosure and the building systems it embodies, in other words, distilled into a gesture of intention. The real challenge comes from carrying this expression throughout the entire architecture process, especially when one practices out of a less developed or less sophisticated context.

Looking back at the last twenty years of finding our own expression, I feel lucky indeed to have the opportunity to create these gestures of architecture. I never thought that I would base my practice in Taiwan, nor expected that we could go this far, with such a diverse range of works, with the freedom that we've enjoyed. Perhaps not ever an architecture hotspot or cradle in any way, Taiwan had presented us with a trust in creativity, spirit of experimentation, daringness to dream and the commitments of clients who want to leave something more lasting or permanent, and of meaning to the next generation. I'm extremely grateful to all my clients and partners who are so willing to go through all the extra miles with us.

All this didn't come easily or effortlessly. The book title "Inspired by constraints" quite fittingly describes the atmosphere of how these projects came to be. It also reflects the challenge of practicing in Taiwan, where dilemma and constraints of politics and identity runs all too real, often on the brink of high tension. With architecture, I often feel as if we are at war, on the front line, if we are to accomplish what/how we want to build, continuously fighting all that is thrown at us, while remaining highly flexible to adapt to myriad complex local contingencies if we are to materialize our ideas "successfully," against odds of entrenched conventions and biases besides the usual budget, schedule and site issues. Of course there have also been many failures which are valuable lessons learnt.

Over the years, we've learnt to have the courage to be different, to be unafraid of not fitting in. The works collected here map our journey, a reminder of where we've been, a milestone from which our own expectations can be further upended in the future.

We strive to design and build with purpose for our clients, our society, and our generation, and to become a small part of the global effort to make our environment better, more human, more emotional, more meaningful one project at a time. Yet architecture is as grounded culturally and physically as the earth it sits on, so our goals and aspirations must be spoken with local means and methods, wherever local happens to be. Formulas and imageries of imported ideas or typologies, needless to say, is weak against the critical honesty we face with every projects. To those who are culturally fluid, like myself and, I believe, countless others with similar background stories to mine, this is about identity, about mental survival.

I wish to extend my deepest gratitude to my amazing team at XRANGE, in particular Jasmine Chen, Sophia Huang, Emily Searchfield Lin and Julie Lin who've been with us through thick and thin, and all the "xrangers" whose hard work and dedication have made all this possible. A note of recognition also goes to all those who have participated on our projects, for you have added significant diversity and energies to the projects. Lastly, I owe all this to Royce Hong, my co-founder, partner and husband, who remains my greatest supporter as well as my toughest critic, your strategic thinking, business acumen, people sense and input have continuously inspired me to challenge myself, to reach beyond, to dream freely.

Appendix

Selected Works Credits

— UNIFYING divergences

Wandering Walls
"ArchDaily Best Architectural Projects of 2022",
"ArchDaily Building of The Year Nominee 2023",
"2022 Rethinking The Future
Awards, Hospitality (built), Third Award"
Location: Hengchun Township, Pingtung County, Taiwan
Program Function: Hospitality
Architecture Design: XRANGE Architects
Landscape Design: XRANGE Architects
Project Team Members: Grace Cheung, Royce Hong, Emily Lin,
Peihsuan Hsu, Jason Chen, Miriam Park, Sonia Pan, Beatrice
Cordella, Edgar Navarrete
Construction Material: RC, slab & bearing wall
Site Area: 2,880 m²
Building Area: 490 m²
Building Height: 10.48 m
No. of Floors: 3 floors on the ground
Design: 2013-2015
Construction: 2016-2019
Completion: 2020.06.01
Consultant
Structural Engineers: Top Technic Engineering Consultants Co., Ltd.
Lighting Design: Unolai Lighting Design & Associates
Photography
Kuo-Min Lee, Lorenzo Pierucci Studio, Studio Millspace

Urban Code Building
Location: Taipei City, Taiwan
Program Function: Housing
Architecture Design: XRANGE Architects
Interior Design: XRANGE Architects
Landscape Design: XRANGE Architects
Project Team Members: Grace Cheung, Royce Hong, Emily Lin, Julie
Lin, Peihsuan Hsu, Jason Jen, Dahwei Wang, Beatrice Cordella,
Miriam Park, Urdaneta Zeberio
Site Area: 433.78 m²
Building Area: 1,585 m²
No. of Floors: 7 floors on the ground and 1 floor underground
Design: 2015-2018
Construction: 2018-2021
Consultant
Structural Engineers: Top Technic Engineering Consultants Co., Ltd.
Lighting Design: Unolai Lighting Design & Associates
Mechanical & Electrical Engineering: Linshen Environmental Control
Design Co., Ltd.
Construction
Construction Co.: Panasonic Homes Taiwan Co., Ltd.
Photography
Kuo-Min Lee, Lorenzo Pierucci Studio, SENSEKON Leo Shih

The Cloud
"2009 I.D. Design Review, Environment category, Design Distinction"
Location: Taipei City, Taiwan
Program Function: Art / Culture
Installation Design: XRANGE Architects
Project Team Members: Grace Cheung, Royce Hong, Yenhao Chen,

Wenting Chao, Yin-ying Tseng, Erika Lu
Floor Area: 300 m²
Design: 2008
Construction: 2008
Consultant
Structural Engineers: Tomita Structural Design
Photography
Marc Geritssen

Winbond Electronics Corporation
Location: Zhubei City, Hsinchu County, Taiwan
Client: Winbond Electronics Corporation
Program Function: Office
Architecture Design: XRANGE Architects, JJP Architects & Planners
Landscape Design: XRANGE Architects, JJP Architects & Planners
Project Team Members: Grace Cheung, Royce Hong, Emily Lin, Julie
Lin, Catherine Kao, Urdaneta Zeberio, Jason Chen, Norince Lee,
Miriam Park, Beatrice Cordella, Sonia Pan, Dahwei Wang, Edgar
Navarrete, Jason Jen
Construction Material: RC, Steel structure
Site Area: 5,000 m²
Building Area: 2,215 m²
Floor Area: 43,000 m²
Building Height: 88.7 m
No. of Floors: 19 floors on the ground and 5 floors underground
Design: 2015-2016
Construction: 2016-2019
Completion: 2020.02
Consultant
Construction Co. : Envision Engineering Consultant
Lighting Design: Unolai Lighting Design & Associates
Wood Structure: Te Feng Lumber Co., Ltd
Mechanical & Electrical Engineering: Majestic Engineering
Consultants Inc
Air Conditioning Engineering: Yuan-Tai Engineering Consulting Co., Ltd.
Construction
Construction Co.: TASA Construction Corporation
Interior Construction: L&L Interiors Inc, TASA Construction
Corporation
Wood Structure: Te Feng Lumber Co., Ltd
Curtain Wall: Mega Facade Corporation
Electrical & Plumbing Engineering: Continental Engineering
Corporation
Fire System Engineering: Continental Engineering Corporation
Air Conditioning Engineering: Continental Engineering Corporation
Photography
Kuo-Min Lee, Lorenzo Pierucci Studio

— LAYERING complexities

Ant Farm House
"2009 The Phaidon Atlas of 21st Century World Architecure"
Location: Taipei City, Taiwan
Program Function: Residential
Architecture Design: XRANGE Architects
Project Team Members: Grace Cheung, Royce Hong, Erika Lu, Dema
Chang, Dorothy Tseng, Yin-ying Tseng

Building Area: 330 m²
Floor Area: 500 m²
No. of Floors: 3 floors on the ground
Design: 2004-2005
Construction: 2005-2006
Consultant
Structural Engineers: Xuzhan Structural Technician Office
Construction
Construction Co.: Xinguang Engineering Co., Ltd.
Photography
Ruan Wei-Min, Scott Morgan

House Of Music
Location: Shilin District, Taipei City, Taiwan
Program Function: Residential
Architecture Design: XRANGE Architects
Project Team Members: Grace Cheung, Royce Hong, Dema Chang, Yin-ying Tseng, Tony Sun, Bert Chen, Yenhao Chen, Dorothy Tseng
Site Area: 150 m²
Floor Area: 250 m²
No. of Floors: 6 floors on the ground
Design: 2007-2008
Construction: 2009-2011
Consultant
Structural Engineers: Neutral Engineering Consultants
Construction
Construction Co.: Fuguach Architecture, Kuoyoa Construction Company
Electrical & Plumbing Engineering: Wantai Industrial Technician Office
Photography
Kuo-Min Lee

Beetle House
Location: Taitung County, Taiwan
Program Function: Residential
Architecture Design: XRANGE Architects
Interior Design: XRANGE Architects
Landscape Design: XRANGE Architects
Project Team Members:
Grace Cheung, Royce Hong, Dema Chang, Tony Chen
Site Area: 300 m²
Design: 2007-2008
Consultant
Structural Engineers: Tomita Structural Design

HAX
Location: Taipei CIty, Taiwan
Program Function: Art / Culture / Industrial
Architecture Design: XRANGE Architects
Project Team Members: Grace Cheung, Royce Hong, Emily Lin, Julie Lin, Jason Lin
Site Area: 1,243 m²
Floor Area: 4,777.02 m²
Design: 2018-

— FORMING abstractions

Stone Cloud

Location: New Taipei City, Taiwan
Program Function: Pavilion
Architecture Design: XRANGE Architects
Project Team Members: Grace Cheung, Royce Hong, Emily Lin, Julie Lin, Melanie Laffay
Site Area: 3,419 m²
Design: Dec 2019
Completion: Feb 2020
Consultant
Structural Engineers: Chungan Wellsun Co., Ltd.
Construction
Metal Fabrication: Jenling Aluminum Co., Ltd.
Photography
Lorenzo Pierucci Studio

Penghu House
"2021 AIA International Design Awards-Merit Awards for Open International | Architecture", "2022 Rethinking The Future Awards, Private Residence (Small-Medium) (Built), First Award"
Location: Penghu County, Taiwan
Program Function: Residential
Architecture Design: XRANGE Architects
Landscape Design: XRANGE Architects
Project Team Members: Grace Cheung, Royce Hong, Emily Lin, Julie Lin, Peihsuan Hsu, Urdaneta Zeberio, Sonia Pan, Miriam Park, Beatrice Cordella, Macarena Azqueta, Chingting Su, Ivan Chen
Construction Material: RC, slab & bearing wall
Site Area: 620 m²
Floor Area: 645 m²
Building Height: 12.2 m
No. of Floors: 3 floors on the ground
Design: 2015-2016
Construction: 2016-2019
Completion: 2020.08
Consultant
Structural Engineers: Top Technic Engineering Consultants Co., Ltd.
Lighting Design: Unolai Lighting Design & Associates
Construction
Construction Co.: Yu Chen Construction Engineering Ltd
Interior Construction: Kwong Fung Interiors Inc
Photography
Kuo-Min Lee, page 146: Central News Agency

Sea Rock
Location: Penghu County, Taiwan
Program Function: Hospitality
Architecture Design: XRANGE Architects
Project Team Members: Grace Cheung, Royce Hong, Emily Lin, Julie Lin, Peihsuan Hsu
Site Area: 6,732.25 m²
Floor Area: 4,040 m²
Design: 2021-

Urban Scope
Location: Taipei City, Taiwan
Client: Taipei City Urban Redevelopment Office
Program Function: Art/ Culture
Architecture Design: XRANGE Architects, Peng Shuangquan Architects
Project Team Members: Grace Cheung, Royce Hong, Erika Lu,

Yenhao Chen, Dema Chang: Shokan Hsieh
Site Area: 23,269m²
Building Area: 880 m²
Design: 2010
Consultant
Structural Engineers: Neutral Engineering Consultants, Tomita Structural Design
Construction
Electrical & Plumbing Engineering: Wantai Industrial Technician Office

Petals
Location: Taitung City, Taiwan
Program Function: Hospitality
Architecture Design: XRANGE Architects
Landscape Design: XRANGE Architects
Project Team Members:
Grace Cheung, Royce Hong, Emily Lin, Julie Lin, Peihsuan Hsu
Site Area: 2,266.87 m²
Floor Area: 3,539.83 m²
Design: 2021-

Landscape Of Traces
"2021 AIA International Design Awards-Commendation for Urban Design", "2022 Rethinking The Future Awards, Public Landscape Project (Built), First Award", "2021 FIABCI-Taiwan Real Estate Excellence Awards, Environment & Culture Category, Golden Quality Award"
Location: Taipei City, Taiwan
Client: National Taiwan Museum
Program Function: Landscape
Landscape Design: XRANGE Architects
Project Team Members: Grace Cheung, Royce Hong, Emily Lin, Peihsuan Hsu, Sonia Pan, Joey Hsieh, Jason Chen, Norince Lee, Haochun Hung, Miriam Park, Soledad Moreno Velasco, Changchun Tsao, Yourue Wang
Site Area: 17,000 m²
Design: 2014-2015
Completion: 2020.07.06
Collaborators
Masterplan architecture/Landscape: B.Y.Hsu Architect
Restoration of Heritage buildings: ZC Architect & Associates
Consultant
Lighting Design: Unolai Lighting Design & Associates
Photography
Studio Millspace, page 211: Huo-Zeng Li / United Daily News Group

— PLAYING tectonics

IPEVO Office
Location: Taipei City, Taiwan
Client: IPEVO Inc.
Program Function: Office
Interior Design: XRANGE Architects
Project Team Members: Grace Cheung, Royce Hong, Peihsuan Hsu, Melanie Laffay
Floor Area: 650 m²
Design: Jan 2020
Completion: Jun 2020
Construction
Interior Contractor: Marvelous Studio
Photography
Lorenzo Pierucci Studio

XING Mobility Workshop
Location: Taipei City, Taiwan
Client: XING Mobility
Program Function: Office/ Workshop

Interior Design: XRANGE Architects
Project Team Members: Grace Cheung, Royce Hong, Emily Lin, Miriam Park, Chingting Su, Dahwei Wang
Floor Area: 650 m²
Design: 2016
Construction: 2016
Construction
Interior Contractor: Marvelous Studio
Photography
Kuo-Min Lee, Lorenzo Pierucci Studio

Gravity Cube/Split Planes
Client: Huang Yi Studio
Program Function: Stage Set
Performance: Huang Yi Studio + "Little Ant & Robot: A Nomad Café"
Stage Set Design: XRANGE Architects
Project Team Members: Grace Cheung, Royce Hong, Emily Lin, Brian Lin
Design: May 2020
Completion: Oct 2021
Construction
Interior Contractor: Marvelous Studio
Gravity Cube Fabrication: Shyang-Shye Enterprise Co., Ltd
Fracture Plane Fabrication: D-fic project engineering Limited company
Photography
Lorenzo Pierucci Studio, page 250: Summer Yen / HUANG YI STUDIO+

C House
Location: Taipei City, Taiwan
Program Function: Residential
Interior Design: XRANGE Architects
Project Team Members: Grace Cheung, Royce Hong, Emily Lin, Starry Wu, Julie Lin, Peihsuan Hsu
Floor Area: 220 m²
Design: Jun 2020
Completion: Aug 2021
Construction
Stair Contractor: Te Feng Lumber Co., Ltd, Shinhand Ltd
Photography
Studio Millspace

Wave Matrix
Location: Taipei City, Taiwan
Program Function: Garage
Architecture Design: XRANGE Architects
Project Team Members: Grace Cheung, Royce Hong, Emily Lin, Yuchun Lin, Kepeng Chang
Floor Area: 113.5 m²
Design: Apr 2019
Completion: Jan 2022
Consultant
Structural Engineers: Chungan Wellsun Co., Ltd.
Construction
Constractor: Shyang-Shye Enterprise Co., Ltd.
Steel Fabrication: Jenling Aluminum Co., Ltd.
Photography
Lorenzo Pierucci Studio

KAPOK
Location: Xinyi District, Taipei City, Taiwan
Client: Kapok, Hong Kong
Program Function: Retail
Interior Design: XRANGE Architects
Project Team Members: Grace Cheung, Royce Hong, Emily Lin
Floor Area: 200 m²
Design: 2014
Completion: May 2014
Photography
Te-Fan Wang

AMBA Hotel
"2012 Wallpaper Magazine Best Business Hotel"
Location: Shimenting, Taipei City, Taiwan
Client: Ambassador Hotel
Program Function: Hospitality
Architecture Design: XRANGE Architects
Project Team Members: Grace Cheung, Royce Hong, Yenhao Chen,
Jony Liu, Erika Lu, Bert Chen
Site Area: 2,169 m^2
Floor Area: 12,455 m^2
Design: 2010-2011
Completion: Feb 2012
Consultant
Structural Engineers: Neutral Engineering Consultants, Lin
Binghong Structural Technician Firm
Lighting Design: Unolai Lighting Design & Associates
Construction
Construction Co.: Songken Construction Engineering Co., Ltd.
Photography
Kuo-Min Lee

CC Hong Memorial Hall
Location: Taipei City, Taiwan
Client: National Electric Appliance Co. Ltd.
Program Function: Education
Interior Design: XRANGE Architects
Project Team Members: Grace Cheung, Royce Hong, Albert Hsu,
Jong Liu
Floor Area: 250 m^2
Design: 2012
Completion: Sep 2012
Construction
Interior Construction: Wei-Hao Interiors Design
Photography
Kuo-Min Lee

Rainbow
Interior Design: XRANGE Architects
Location: Taipei City, Taiwan
Program Function: Residential
Construction Material: eco resin, stainless steel
Size: 500 cm L* 200 cm W* 250 cm H

Playpath
Location: Taipei city, Taiwan
Program Function: Landscape
Landscape Design: XRANGE Architects
Project Team Members: Grace Cheung, Royce Hong, Emily Lin, Julie
Lin, Peihsuan Hsu, Yuchun Lin, Malanie Laffay
Site Area: 7,550 m^2
Design: 2019-

Firm profile

XRANGE Architects

XRANGE was founded 2003 in Taipei by architect Grace Cheung and industrial designer and serial entrepreneur Royce YC Hong. XRANGE works on multiple scales, with a scope and diversity of projects encompassing masterplans, architecture, landscape, installations and products.

Steered by the founders' extensive international background and cultural fluency, XRANGE's work is characterized by concise strategic thinking, bold forms and distinctive material attitude shaped by local contexts. Inspired by constraints unique to every project, XRANGE's architecture strives for original solutions that create meaning and place for users. With unwavering commitment to purpose and performance, XRANGE takes an essential and adaptive design approach, capitalizing on minimal means to realize works that are grounded without compromising human and environmental factors, spatial experience, design innovation and the soul of craft.

The work of XRANGE has been exhibited and published in numerous international platforms and media. Cheung was awarded two AIA International Design Awards for both architecture and urban design in 2021.

Sukching Grace Cheung AIA
Principal Architect

Founder and Principal Architect of XRANGE. Holding a Master of Architecture from Columbia University, Cheung is a USA licensed architect living and practicing in Taipei. Prior to co-founding XRANGE, Cheung gained her experience in top offices around the world, at Patkau Architects in Vancouver, Bernard Tschumi Architects in New York and OMA (Office for Metropolitan Architecture) Asia in Hong Kong and Rotterdam.

Born in Malaysia before moving to Canada in her teens, Cheung has lived, studied and worked on 3 continents: America, Europe and Asia. Seeing herself as a front-line worker in the shifting cultural contexts that shaped her and characterized her practice, Cheung brings her cultural fluency and international background to steer XRANGE towards a specifically localized yet global critical point of view with the methods and materials of architecture.

A TEDxTaipei speaker, Cheung has taught at multiple universities and is a frequent lecturer, guest critic and juror both in her adopted home Taiwan and abroad. Cheung is also the Vice Chairman and Executive Director of the Hong Foundation, extending its five decade philanthropic legacy synonymous with the social and cultural heritage of Taiwan into the next wave.

Architect CV / Biography
Sukching Grace Cheung (Registered Architect, California, USA)
Co-Founder and Principal Architect of XRANGE Architects

Education
Master of Architecture, Columbia University, New York, USA (1994)

Experience
Patkau Architects of Vancouver (1993),
Bernard Tschumi Architects of New York (1994),
Senior Associate of OMA (Office of Metropolitan Architecture) Asia in Hong Kong & Rotterdam (1995-2000)

Book credits

Art Direction by Oscar Riera Ojeda.
Graphic Design by Lucía B. Bauzá.
Copy Editing by Kit Maude & Michael W. Phillips Jr.

OSCAR RIERA OJEDA
PUBLISHERS

Copyright 2023 Oscar Riera Ojeda Publishers Limited
ISBN 978-1-946226-86-0
Published by Oscar Riera Ojeda Publishers Limited
Printed in China

Oscar Riera Ojeda Publishers Limited
Unit 1331, Beverley Commercial Centre,
87-105 Chatham Road South, Tsim Sha Tsui, Kowloon, Hong Kong

Production Offices
Suit 19, Shenyun Road,
Nanshan District, Shenzhen 518055, China

International Customer Service & Editorial Questions: +1-484-502-5400

www.oropublishers.com | www.oscarrieraojeda.com
oscar@oscarrieraojeda.com